WEB GRAPHICS

in easy

MARY LOJKINE

COMPUTER
STEP

In easy steps is an imprint of Computer Step
Southfield Road . Southam
Warwickshire CV47 0FB . England

http://www.ineasysteps.com

Notice of Liability
Every effort has been made to ensure that this book contains accurate and current information. However, Computer Step and the author shall not be liable for any loss or damage suffered by readers as a result of any information contained herein.

Trademarks
All trademarks are acknowledged as belonging to their respective companies.

Printed and bound in the United Kingdom

ISBN 1-84078-231-5

Contents

9 Panoramas 165

10 Images for e-mail 177

Index 187

First things first

On the Web, image is (almost) everything. This chapter explains what graphics do and why they matter, and the differences between good and bad design. It also covers the software and hardware you'll need to get started.

Covers

Chapter One

Image is (almost) everything

The Internet was born in 1969, but it didn't come of age until the early 1990s, when the World Wide Web appeared. Before the Web, the Internet belonged to computer specialists. If you didn't have the technical know-how to get connected, the patience to find and configure the software and the imagination to think of an application for it, you didn't use the Internet. When the Web took off, the Internet became popular with everyone, from business people with fancy laptops to children logging on at school.

The Web introduced two great new concepts: it was easy to use and it had pictures (graphics, in computer terms). If you've ever struggled with a computer, you'll know that ease of use can be the difference between getting the job done and stomping off to do something else. Pictures might not seem as important, but they're a big part of the Web's popularity.

Think of the difference between radio and television: people listen to the radio while they're working or travelling, but they don't sit down around it for an evening's entertainment. Television is more absorbing. And how about newspapers? You used to get columns of text, but now there are photographs and diagrams, colour supplements and weekend magazines. Still not convinced? Look at these two Web pages and decide which one you'd read first.

On the Web, graphics draw people in and encourage them to browse. They can attract attention, break up the text, illustrate points that would be difficult to explain in words, create an identity for the site, help with navigation… or do all of the above.

Graphics for information

The most obvious use for a graphic is to show people what something looks like. Adding a photograph to a Web page is easier than using words to describe a person, place or product.

Examples of 'information' graphics include:

- Photographs accompanying articles and travelogues. You can rave about the blue sky, white sand and crystal-clear waters, but adjectives such as 'beautiful' and 'idyllic' mean different things to different people. A picture says it all

- Product photographs on shopping Web sites. Even though people can't handle the merchandise, they still want to see what they're getting – not least so they can be sure they're ordering the right thing

- Step-by-step photographs or drawings explaining how to make or assemble something. The picture-only instructions that come with kitset furniture might not seem helpful, but imagine how much worse they'd be if they only used words

- Maps showing how to find a town or building. A map can be more useful than an address, especially if it includes the nearby landmarks

- Charts and graphs on financial Web sites. If you want people to see the trends, turn your tables of data into charts

Graphics for style

Graphics can also decorate and structure a Web site. Design elements such as logos, buttons and backgrounds are known as Web-page 'furniture' because they create a 'home' for the content.

'Style' graphics serve many purposes:

- They give your Web site a visual identity, making it easy to recognise and separating it from other sites. You want people to know where they are when they reach your site, and to notice when a link takes them away

- They help people find their way around. If you use the same buttons throughout your site, visitors soon learn how they work. You can also use distinctive logos or backgrounds to divide the site into sections

- They divide the text into manageable chunks, making it more approachable and easier to read

- They create an atmosphere that reflects the content, be it light-hearted, edgy, serious, romantic or sombre

- They make the site attractive, encouraging people to browse

Looks aren't everything, but they certainly matter. With millions of Web sites to choose from, people are more likely to spend time on a good-looking one. They're more likely to remember it and more likely to return. Sites that look good also get more publicity in computer magazines and other 'real world' publications.

Information or style?

You should think about the purpose of each graphic, because it affects the decisions you make about size, colours, compression and file format. If you're using a picture to convey information, it may be important to preserve all the details. If it's there to add style, you might be able to simplify it.

Everything on your Web pages should serve some purpose. If you don't know why you've included a graphic, delete it!

All your own work

There are lots of ways to design a Web site. People in huge corporations employ a design agency. People in medium-sized companies hire a designer. Since you bought this book, you probably want to create your own site.

You could get your graphics from a clip-art disc, but it's much better to design your own. That way, they'll be unique and distinctive, and you'll get exactly what you want. You can choose the size, the colour and the style.

Web graphics in easy steps is all about creating graphics and adding them to your Web pages. It's divided into three sections:

'HTML' is short for 'HyperText Mark-up Language'. You'll learn more about it in Chapter 3.

- Chapters 1 to 3 provide background information. They deal with design issues, software practicalities, the fundamentals of image files and the basics of HTML, the language used to create and format Web pages

- Chapters 4 to 7 are hands-on chapters that get you designing graphics, working with photographs and creating Web pages. They cover everything from simple logos and buttons to interactive images and clever tricks to improve your layout

- Chapters 8, 9 and 10 deal with three specialised applications: animations, 360-degree panoramas and graphics for e-mail

Each of the first seven chapters builds on information from the previous ones. The last three chapters can be explored at your leisure, as you need the techniques.

Some of the information in Chapters 2 and 3 may not seem important at first. Don't worry if you can't see the point of every detail or remember all the different file types and HTML tags – things will become clear when you start designing. As you get more experienced, you can refer back to these chapters. Practical experience makes the theory easier to grasp, and understanding the theory makes the practical work easier and more effective.

You should be able to create all the graphics for a basic Web site by the end of Chapter 5.

Good design

You might feel like Picasso when you run your graphics program, but you aren't making art, you're designing. There's an important difference: artists can do what they want, but designers have to stick to their brief.

Your graphics have to work together to enhance your Web site, so you need to follow a few basic rules. Every graphic should download quickly and be appropriate, accessible and simple.

Quick to download

If there's one thing Web users hate, it's pages… that… appear… very… slowly. Making trade-offs to keep your pages moving is the single most important aspect of designing Web graphics.

For an individual graphic, the download time depends on file size, which in turn depends on the size and nature of the image. However, the download time for an entire Web page depends on the total amount of data, so a page with many small images can take longer to download than a page with a single large one.

Appropriate

Images should not only suit the Web site, but also the audience and their hardware.

Making images appropriate to the site is easy. Think about your subject: are the graphics related to it in some way? For example, you might create ball and racquet icons for a tennis site, or use tins of paint on a site about DIY. More usually, you have to choose a style and colour that suit your material. For example, the Royal Family's official Web site is formal and traditional, whereas Victoria Beckham's has colourful cartoons.

Find these Web sites at http://www.royal.co.uk/ *and* http://www.victoriabeckham.mu/ *respectively.*

Matching your graphics to your audience involves more guesswork. It's a fair bet that business people have less patience than people using the Internet for entertainment, so they'll appreciate simpler graphics that download quickly. Older people may not be comfortable with the high-tech graphics that appeal to teenagers. If you're aiming your site at artists or designers, looks are everything.

Your audience's hardware is important because it sets the limits for size and colours. People who play computer games or work with digital images have big monitors and powerful graphics cards, so they can display anything you create. People in offices and schools usually have less powerful machines with smaller screens, so they'll appreciate smaller, simpler graphics.

Accessible

Avoid frustrating or excluding potential visitors with poor design. Make sure there's good contrast between text and its background, so it's easy to read. Don't use red on green, which is difficult for everyone and impossible for people who are colour-blind. Avoid complicated backgrounds and excessively small text.

Adding alternative text to your graphics (see page 56) helps people who choose not to display them, perhaps because their connection is slow. It also makes them accessible to blind and partially sighted visitors who rely on text-to-speech convertors.

Avoid specialised image formats that require extra software, because most people won't bother installing it.

Simple

You don't need artistic ability or formal design training to create an attractive site. When in doubt, just keep things simple.

The quickest way to create a mess is by overdesigning your pages. You don't need six styles of button on five different backgrounds, with multicoloured lines and animated logos to top things off. The most important thing on your site is the content, not the incidental graphics, so be restrained. Less is better than more.

Software

You don't need a lot of software to create a Web site and you certainly don't need expensive software. You can get started with just two programs: an image editor and an HTML editor. You may need some utilities later on, but they shouldn't cost much either.

Image editor

You'll need an image-editing program to produce logos, buttons and backgrounds, and to edit and resize photographs.

There are two features your image editor must have:

- The ability to specify the size of an image in pixels (see page 21), rather than inches or centimetres, and to change its size

- Support for the GIF and JPEG image formats

Other useful features include:

- Tools for creating buttons and drop shadows

- Rulers, guidelines and/or a background grid so you can keep everything lined up

- Layers, the computer equivalent of sheets of acetate. They are useful for adding text to buttons – if you place the text on a separate layer that sits over the top, you can edit the text without affecting the underlying button

- Tools for creating interactive image maps and rollovers, and for slicing images into several pieces

- Support for GIF transparency and GIF animation

The graphics in this book were created using Paint Shop Pro. Developed by Jasc Software, it's a popular choice because it's inexpensive but capable. You can download a trial version from Jasc's Web site at http://www.jasc.com/

You can adapt the step-by-step guides in Chapters 4 to 7 for use with other image editors. Some of the tools and options may have different names or be in different places, but the same principles and techniques can be applied.

HTML editor

An HTML editor helps you combine your graphics with text to create Web pages.

Thanks to the popularity of the Web, you can design Web pages using almost anything: a simple text editor, a word processor, a desktop-publishing program or even a graphics program. Then again, that's like saying you can boil water using a camp fire, an electric stove, a microwave, your car's radiator or a thermonuclear reactor. You can, but when you want a cup of tea, you reach for the kettle. An HTML editor is the best tool for creating Web pages because it's optimised for that particular job.

'WYSIWYG' is short for 'What You See Is What You Get'. It's used to describe programs where the screen display (What You See) matches the final output (What You Get).

Some HTML editors show you how your Web pages will look, enabling you to design and edit them visually. If you want to make a headline red, you select it and click a button. This type of program is called is a 'visual' or 'WYSIWYG' HTML editor. The alternative is a program that concentrates on the underlying code, forcing you to learn HTML and add the formatting by hand (see Chapter 3). In general, you're better off with a visual HTML editor, but you may occasionally want to edit the code by hand – for example, to create special effects. Most visual editors also let you do this, so you can combine the two approaches.

The Web pages in this book were created using Namo WebEditor from Namo Interactive. Like Paint Shop Pro, it's powerful but comparatively inexpensive. You can download a trial version from the Web site at `http://www.namo.com/`

HTML is HTML, no matter which program you use to produce it, so you can use the same techniques with other HTML editors.

Utility programs

There are many small programs that can assist you with specific tasks. Over time you'll build up quite a collection.

- **FTP (File Transfer Protocol) program.** The first thing to get is an FTP program. You'll need it to transfer your Web pages from your hard disk to your Web server

- **Webcam program.** If you want to display live images from a Webcam (see page 117), you'll need a utility that captures the images and uploads them. You'll probably get one with your camera

- **Icon editor.** Icons are saved in a special format that few image editors support. If you want to create an icon for your Web site (see page 136), you'll need an icon editor or a utility that can convert ordinary graphics into icon files

- **Animation program.** You may be able to create animated GIFs with your image editor. If you can't, you'll need a specialist animation program (see page 157)

- **Stitching program.** Some image editors can stitch photos together to create panoramic images (see page 167), but most can't – in which case you'll need a standalone program

All these extra programs can be obtained as and when you need them. Most are inexpensive and can be purchased on-line.

Hardware

Apart from a computer, there are three pieces of hardware that are useful for creating Web graphics:

- **Digital cameras** make it easy to add photographs to your Web site. They're especially handy when time is of the essence. If a famous person visits your company, you can add their picture to your Web site within hours. Digital cameras are also great for the artistically challenged. Instead of creating graphics from scratch, you can photograph simple objects and use them as the basis for your designs. The main drawback is that digital cameras are still quite expensive

Nikon's Coolpix 4500

- **Scanners** are cheaper than digital cameras but enable you to do all the same things, albeit more slowly. You have to take a photograph, get your film developed and then scan the print. On the plus side, you may already have snapshots you'd like to use on your Web site, in which case a scanner is the right tool for the job. You can also scan drawings, memorabilia, fabric, leaves and even small objects

- **Webcams** are basic video cameras that only work when they are connected to a computer. They are used to capture live images of your surroundings (see page 117). Webcams work best when you have a spectacular or interesting view to share with other Internet users, but you can point them at anything (and people do). At a pinch, they can also be used to take snapshots of people or objects

Logitech's QuickCam Pro 3000

Web space

Once you've designed your Web pages, you'll need to transfer them to a computer that's permanently connected to the Internet.

Most Internet service providers give you some space on their Web server as part of your account. Check whether there are any conditions attached – you may only be able to use it for a personal, non-commercial Web site. Often there's a limit to the amount of traffic you can receive, which might be a problem if your site becomes very popular.

You also need to find out how to access your Web space. The Support section of your service provider's Web site should have the details. The two important things to know are the procedure for uploading your pages and the address of your site, which will be something like:

```
http://www.username.yourisp.co.uk/
http://www.yourisp.co.uk/username/
```

One detail to look for is the correct filename for the main page of your site. If someone types your Web address without specifying a particular page, most Web servers automatically look for a file called `index.htm` and instruct the browser to display it. Some servers look for `default.htm` instead.

If you're creating a large or commercial Web site, you may need more Web space than your service provider offers. There are many Web-hosting companies that can provide anything from a few megabytes of space to an entire Web server. They will also help you register a domain name, so you can change your Web address to something like:

```
http://www.yourname.co.uk/
```

Check the advertisements in Internet magazines for details.

Image files

This chapter provides background information about image files. It explains how factors such as the number of colours, compression factor and file format determine how your graphics look and how quickly they download.

Covers

Chapter Two

Introduction

Designing Web graphics involves making compromises. You want your pages to look good, but you also want them to download quickly. You want interactivity, but you also want a site everyone can access. You want the 'wow' factor, not the 'ow' factor.

To make the right choices, you need to know how computers store and display images. If you understand the basics, you can work out the best way to save each file. If you don't, you'll end up with graphics that don't look right or are unnecessarily large.

The size of an image file depends on four things:

- Size of the image, in pixels

- Number of colours

- Amount of compression

- File format

These factors also affect the quality of the image. They determine how sharp it is, how much detail you can see and how smooth the shading is – in short, how good it looks. As you might expect, settings that minimise the file size also reduce the quality. The trick is to find the middle ground.

This chapter provides the information you'll need to make the right choices. Skim through it to get an overview of the issues, then come back to it when you have some graphics to experiment with. Some of the concepts are easier to understand when you're sitting in front of your computer, working on an image file.

Bitmap graphics

Most of the graphics on the Web are bitmaps – images made up of rows of tiny coloured squares, arranged in a grid. The squares are known as 'picture elements' or 'pixels'. Normally they are so small that they blend together, but if you get very close to your monitor, you may be able to make them out. Alternatively, use your image editor's Zoom tool to magnify a small section of an image.

Computers don't always store graphics as bitmaps. Drawing programs record lines and shapes mathematically, creating a vector image. Web browsers can't display vector images, so they aren't normally used on Web pages.

One exception is animations created with Macromedia Flash. They often incorporate vector graphics, so you need extra software to display them. The Flash Player interprets the file and sends the images to your screen.

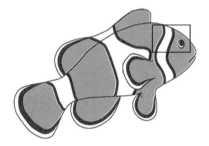

When you save a bitmap graphic, your computer records the colour of each pixel. The more pixels there are, the more data it has to record, and thus the larger the file.

There are two things to remember about pixels:

- Each pixel can only be one colour. You can't have a pixel that's half black and half white

- Pixels are square. This causes problems when an image has diagonal lines or smooth curves (see page 34)

File size

There are two ways to measure the size of a graphic:

- **Pixel size** is the width and height of the graphic when it is displayed on the screen, measured in pixels

- **File size** is the amount of space required when the file is saved on to your hard disk, measured in kilobytes (K)

Pixel size = 300x200
File size = 4.7K

It's important to distinguish between the two sizes when you're discussing images. If someone says a graphic is too large, they might mean it doesn't fit on their screen (pixel size), or they might mean it takes a long time to download (file size). Find out exactly what the problem is before you make any changes!

If you work with printed images, you'll be used to thinking about their resolution – the number of dots per inch in the printed version. On the Web, a pixel in the file becomes a pixel on the screen, so resolution isn't relevant. If your image editor requires you to choose a resolution when you create a new file, select 72dpi – the approximate resolution of a computer screen.

Pixel size affects file size. More pixels means more data, which in general means a bigger file. However, there are other factors that affect file size, including the number of colours, the amount of compression and the file format. Graphics that look smaller on the screen don't necessarily spring from smaller files, and vice versa. For example, the small fish (right) has fewer pixels than the large one (above), but it has many more colours, resulting in a larger file.

Pixel size: 150x100
File size: 10.6K

File size and download time

The bigger the file, the longer it takes to download. It's a simple problem: you can only shift so much data per second, so the more data there is, the longer it takes to transfer the file.

Internet users are impatient people who want Web pages to flash on to their screens in seconds, so large files are a bad thing.

However, there's more to maximising throughput than simply reducing the size of your files.

First, the total download time for a Web page depends on the total amount of data to be transferred. A page with lots of teeny tiny image files on it can download just as slowly as a page with one large image file. If anything, the page with the small files will take longer, because very small files aren't transferred as efficiently. Don't get so focused on individual files that you forget to consider the total image load on each page.

Eight small photos, total 17.5K

One large photo, 15.9K

Second, when your Web browser downloads an image file, it copies it into the cache – a temporary storage area on your hard disk. If you download another Web page that requires the same image, your browser gets it from the cache. You don't have to download it again, so the page appears more quickly.

From a designer's point of view, the benefit of caching is that images that appear on every page of your site, such as navigation buttons, only have to be downloaded once. Try to reuse basic graphics such as rules and bullets throughout your Web site, rather than designing new ones for every page. Also, when you're adding up the image load on a page, you can ignore images that should already be in the user's cache.

Colours

Computers produce colours by mixing red, green and blue light. That may sound strange if you're used to mixing paints or inks, where the primary colours are blue, red and yellow (or cyan, magenta and yellow, for professional printing), but it's correct.

Everything is reversed when you work with light:

- Red plus green gives yellow

- Red plus blue gives pink (magenta)

- Green plus blue gives pale blue (cyan)

The more of each colour you add, the paler the final colour. If you combine red, green and blue light at full strength, you get white (an easy way to remember this is to think about what happens if you combine no red light with no green light and no blue light – you must get black, which is the opposite of white).

When computers store colours, they record the amount of red, green and blue required to mix them. Most computers can make thousands or millions of colours, so storing the 'recipe' is more efficient than having a name for each shade.

The number of colours a computer can make depends on how closely it can control the light. These days, most computers have 256 levels of red to choose from, ranging from completely off to completely on. When the 256 reds are combined with 256 greens and 256 blues, 16,777,216 different colours can be produced. That's more colours than the human eye can distinguish, so it's enough to display photographs accurately.

A 'bit' is the smallest unit of data that a computer can store. Collect together eight bits and you have a 'byte'. A 'kilobyte' (K) contains 1,024 bytes; a 'megabyte' contains 1,024 kilobytes.

It takes eight bits to store a number between zero and 255 (giving 256 levels, when you include zero). There are three 'ingredients' in each recipe, so 24 bits of data are required for each colour and this mixing system is known as '24-bit colour'. Since most people don't know their bits from their bytes, but do want their colours to look right, it's also known, somewhat more helpfully, as 'TrueColor'. Either way, the computer has 16.7 million colours to choose from, so you get subtle gradations and smooth shading.

Indexed colour

When people first started transferring images over the Internet, modems were slow, memory was expensive and most computers had 256-colour displays. Allocating 24 bits of data to each pixel produced image files that were pointlessly large.

Indexed colour is also known as 'paletted colour' because the files contain a palette of colours.

Indexed colour is used for images with up to 256 colours. It's more complicated than 24-bit colour, but it produces smaller files that download more quickly. It works like this:

- Each image file begins with a 'palette' that stores the recipes for up to 256 colours. Each colour is assigned a number

- Instead of storing detailed colour information for each pixel, the file records the corresponding palette numbers

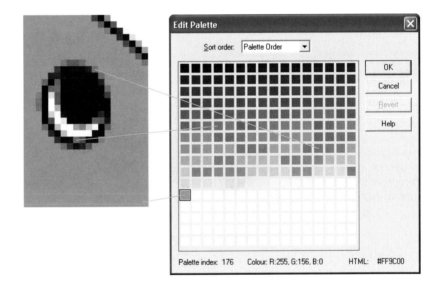

- The palette numbers range from zero to 255, so you need eight bits of data to record the colour of each pixel. This system is known as '8-bit colour' or 'indexed colour'

The advantage of the palette system is that although each image can only contain 256 colours, you (or your software) can choose the best 256 shades from the 16.7 million colours your computer can mix. For example, the palette for the fish graphic contains blacks and oranges, plus some blues and greys to smooth off the edges.

The palette doesn't have to contain 256 colours. For a simple graphic, you might use a palette with 128, 64, 32, 16, eight or four colours. For a black-and-white image (with no greys), a two-colour palette will do. Reducing the number of colours shrinks the file.

256-colour palette, 38K

64-colour palette, 25K

16-colour palette, 14K

Eight-colour palette, 10K

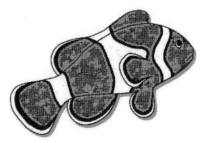

Four-colour palette, 6.4K

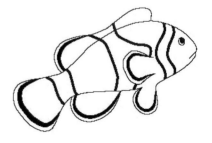

Two-colour palette, 2.3K

Dithering

Indexed colour works well for simple graphics that don't need many colours. Problems can arise with more complicated images such as photographs. Things can also go wrong when you try to display two or more graphics with different palettes.

Most photographs contain thousands of colours. If you try to save them as 256-colour images, your software has to simulate the missing shades. It does this by finding the closest colours in the palette and arranging them in patterns. From a distance, the eye is fooled and you think you're seeing a solid colour. This trick is called 'dithering'.

Actual pixels

Seen from a distance

Dithering is also used by older computers that can only display 256 colours at a time. When they encounter images with thousands or millions of colours, they simulate the extra ones using the colours they have available.

Dithering is most obvious in images that have areas of flat colour, with no shading or texture. It is less obvious in photographs.

Things can go horribly wrong when an older computer has to display several graphics at once. Even if all the images use 256-colour palettes, they may not all use the same palette, so the computer has to work out a compromise. It imposes a standard palette on all the images and uses dithering to recreate the missing shades. Sometimes this works well, but sometimes you end up with speckly patterns that detract from your graphics.

The Web palette

When an older computer with a 256-colour display has to dither graphics on a Web page, it doesn't look at all the files and apply a palette that gives good results. Instead, it automatically uses a special palette that is built in to the Web browser. Microsoft's palette is slightly different from Netscape's, and the Macintosh versions aren't quite the same as the Windows ones, but all four palettes have 216 colours in common. This set of standard colours is known as the 'Web' or 'browser-safe' palette.

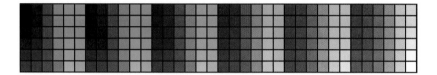

The important thing about the colours in the Web palette is that they don't dither on 256-colour displays. If your image is supposed to have solid colours, that's what you get.

Any old shade of orange   Orange from the Web palette

Most image editors and HTML editors have a built-in Web palette. To choose a browser-safe colour, you call up the palette and click an appropriate shade. Most image editors can also apply the Web palette to an existing image, automatically replacing any 'unsafe' colours with the colours from the palette (see page 76).

If you want to mix the colours yourself, using your image editor's colour picker, there are two simple rules to follow:

- If you make colours by specifying the levels of red, green and blue, the only values you can use are 0, 51, 102, 153, 204 and 255. For example, R=255, G=153, B=51 gives the browser-safe orange from the opposite page

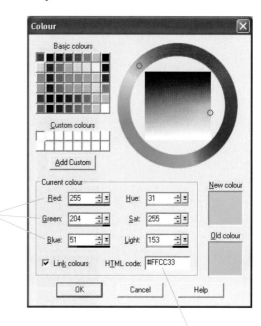

'Hex' is short for 'hexadecimal', a counting system that uses base 16 (rather than base 10, like the normal counting system). Hex is too geeky for everyday life, but it's used to specify colours in HTML. The hex values that produce browser-safe colours are easier to remember than the corresponding RGB values. You don't have to understand hex to use the hex values – you just have to key them in.

- If you make colours by specifying hex values, the only values you can use are 00, 33, 66, 99, CC and FF. Using this system, the orange is FF9933. The hex values for the 216 browser-safe colours are given overleaf

The problem with the Web palette is that the colours were chosen mathematically, rather than aesthetically. There are plenty of bright colours, but relatively few pale ones. Also, there are more cool colours (blues and greens) than warm ones (reds, oranges and yellows). It's easy to find a cool, dark colour for a headline, but there aren't many pale, warm colours you can use behind it.

Browser-safe colours

Here's a reference table showing all the browser-safe colours, with their corresponding hex values. If your image editor doesn't have a built-in Web palette, you can use it to choose colours.

#000000	#003300	#006600	#009900	#00CC00	#00FF00
#000033	#003333	#006633	#009933	#00CC33	#00FF33
#000066	#003366	#006666	#009966	#00CC66	#00FF66
#000099	#003399	#006699	#009999	#00CC99	#00FF99
#0000CC	#0033CC	#0066CC	#0099CC	#00CCCC	#00FFCC
#0000FF	#0033FF	#0066FF	#0099FF	#00CCFF	#00FFFF
#330000	#333300	#336600	#339900	#33CC00	#33FF00
#330033	#333333	#336633	#339933	#33CC33	#33FF33
#330066	#333366	#336666	#339966	#33CC66	#33FF66
#330099	#333399	#336699	#339999	#33CC99	#33FF99
#3300CC	#3333CC	#3366CC	#3399CC	#33CCCC	#33FFCC
#3300FF	#3333FF	#3366FF	#3399FF	#33CCFF	#33FFFF
#660000	#663300	#666600	#669900	#66CC00	#66FF00
#660033	#663333	#666633	#669933	#66CC33	#66FF33
#660066	#663366	#666666	#669966	#66CC66	#66FF66
#660099	#663399	#666699	#669999	#66CC99	#66FF99
#6600CC	#6633CC	#6666CC	#6699CC	#66CCCC	#66FFCC
#6600FF	#6633FF	#6666FF	#6699FF	#66CCFF	#66FFFF

Some of the colours – particularly the greens – will look slightly different on your screen, because it isn't possible to reproduce all the screen colours with printing inks.

#990000	#993300	#996600	#999900	#99CC00	#99FF00
#990033	#993333	#996633	#999933	#99CC33	#99FF33
#990066	#993366	#996666	#999966	#99CC66	#99FF66
#990099	#993399	#996699	#999999	#99CC99	#99FF99
#9900CC	#9933CC	#9966CC	#9999CC	#99CCCC	#99FFCC
#9900FF	#9933FF	#9966FF	#9999FF	#99CCFF	#99FFFF
#CC0000	#CC3300	#CC6600	#CC9900	#CCCC00	#CCFF00
#CC0033	#CC3333	#CC6633	#CC9933	#CCCC33	#CCFF33
#CC0066	#CC3366	#CC6666	#CC9966	#CCCC66	#CCFF66
#CC0099	#CC3399	#CC6699	#C9999	#CCCC99	#CCFF99
#CC00CC	#CC33CC	#CC66CC	#CC99CC	#CCCCCC	#CCFFCC
#CC00FF	#CC33FF	#CC66FF	#CC99FF	#CCCCFF	#CCFFFF
#FF0000	#FF3300	#FF6600	#FF9900	#FFCC00	#FFFF00
#FF0033	#FF3333	#FF6633	#FF9933	#FFCC33	#FFFF33
#FF0066	#FF3366	#FF6666	#FF9966	#FFCC66	#FFFF66
#FF0099	#FF3399	#FF6699	#FF9999	#FFCC99	#FFFF99
#FF00CC	#FF33CC	#FF66CC	#FF99CC	#FFCCCC	#FFFFCC
#FF00FF	#FF33FF	#FF66FF	#FF99FF	#FFCCFF	#FFFFFF

Playing it safe

You don't have to use browser-safe colours for all your graphics. These days most people have computers that can display thousands or millions of colours, rather than just 256. Your graphics won't dither on their screens, no matter what colours you use.

There are some situations where it is still advisable to pick colours from the browser-safe palette:

- For page backgrounds, text and links

- For logos, buttons, bullets and rules

- For illustrations that have large areas of flat colour

Simple graphics look terrible with dithered colours. The patterns are very obvious and distracting, because there isn't much else for the eye to focus on. There's no reason *not* to use browser-safe colours for these items, and doing so ensures they'll look right for everyone, regardless of the age of their computer.

You can't use the Web palette for graphics with shading or drop shadows, because it doesn't have enough shades of any particular colour to give you smooth transitions. You'll have to save them as 256-colour images, using a palette that provides all the necessary shades. However, you might still want to choose browser-safe colours for areas that aren't shaded, such as the body of the fish.

216-colour Web palette   256-colour palette

Don't use the Web palette for photographs. They should be saved as 24-bit images.

Transparency

One of the colours in the palette can be made transparent. When the graphic is used on a Web page, the background shows through the transparent areas. It looks as if the graphic is an irregular shape, although in fact it's still a rectangle, with see-through areas around the edge. You can also have transparent areas in the middle, so the background can show through the centre of an 'A' or 'O'.

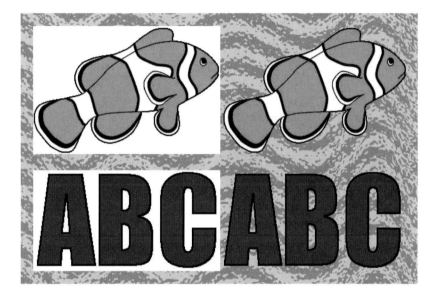

White background   Transparent background

Transparency is useful when you want to place a graphic on several pages with different backgrounds. To find out how to create transparent images, see page 141.

Anti-aliasing

Pixels are square pegs, which is unfortunate when you're trying to draw a round hole. There's no easy way to create a smooth curve or a diagonal line when your building blocks are square.

Anti-aliasing is a partial solution. It softens the edges of curved or diagonal lines by adding pixels of an intermediate colour. If you're drawing a black line on a white background, anti-aliasing adds grey pixels along the edges. Your eye blends everything together and the line looks smoother.

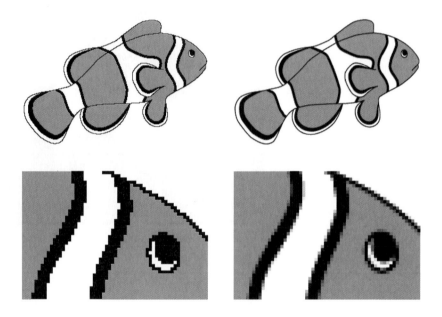

Without anti-aliasing   With anti-aliasing

Most image editors add anti-aliasing automatically. Usually that's what you want, but sometimes you'll need to turn off this option. Anti-aliasing has three drawbacks:

- It isn't as effective when you're using the Web palette

- It increases the size of the image file (see page 37)

- It can't be used along the edges of images with transparent backgrounds

Colour cheat sheet

So far you've encountered three colour systems: 24-bit colour, indexed colour and indexed colour with the Web palette. Here's a quick summary of what they provide and when to use them:

Drawings, cartoons, diagrams, maps and charts all count as illustrations.

System	Colours	Applications
24-bit colour (TrueColor)	16.7 million	Photographs, illustrations with many colours or sophisticated shading
Indexed colour	Palette of 256, chosen from 16.7 million available shades	Most illustrations, including those with anti-aliasing, shading or drop shadows
Indexed colour with Web palette	Palette of 216, all standard shades	Backgrounds, text, Web-page furniture, simple illustrations with areas of flat colour

Chapter 4 explains how to choose the right colour system when you create an image, and also how to adjust the number of colours before you save it.

Images at the ends of the scale are easy to deal with. Photographs should be saved as 24-bit images. Basic items of Web-page furniture, such as logos and simple buttons, should be designed using colours from the Web palette.

Finding the right colour system for an illustration can be a matter of trial and error. If you created it using your image editor's default settings, it's probably a 24-bit image. Apply the Web palette and see how it looks. If your attractive drawing becomes an ugly mess, select the Undo option and turn it into a 256-colour image. If it looks okay, try reducing the number of colours. If it doesn't, you'll have to save it as a 24-bit image.

Some image editors can display side-by-side previews of all the options, making it easier to pick the right settings.

Compression

File compression is all about storing data efficiently, so it takes up less space. It's the computer equivalent of keeping a small suitcase inside a larger one, rather than alongside it.

Compression can make a dramatic difference to the size of your image files. Without compression, it would be impossible to add photographs to your Web site. The files would be so large that people wouldn't be willing to wait for them to download.

600x400 pixels
Uncompressed size: 720K

600x400 pixels
Compressed size: 23K

Even simple graphics such as buttons and bullets benefit from compression. The smaller the file, the more quickly it downloads.

Compression usually involves looking for patterns and finding ways to store them. There are two approaches:

- **Lossless compression** condenses the data without changing the appearance of the graphic in any way

- **Lossy compression** changes the graphic so the data can be condensed even further. You lose detail and smoothness

Lossy compression usually gives smaller files than lossless compression. However, it depends on the image.

LZW compression

LZW compression was developed by Abraham Lempel, Jakob Ziv and Terry Welch (hence 'LZW'). LZW compression is lossless, so it doesn't change the appearance of your graphic.

The LZW algorithm looks for repeating patterns across the horizontal rows of pixels. It draws up a list of patterns and then uses it like a palette. When a pattern appears, the data is replaced by a reference to the list.

File size: 0.2K   File size: 0.6K   File size: 3.0K   File size: 13K

The first image has two very simple horizontal patterns. Some rows contain 100 orange pixels (pattern one – p1) and some contain 100 blue ones (pattern two – p2). Instead of recording the colour of each pixel, the compressed file stores the pattern for each row: p1, p1, p1, p1, p1, p2, p2, p2, p2, p2, p1, p1... and so on. Because it is very simple, this file compresses very well.

The second image has a slightly more complicated horizontal pattern, so the file is a little bigger. In the third image, the patterns have been disrupted. There are more colours, because the curved lines are anti-aliased, and the file is harder to compress.

The fourth image also has random variations in colour – adjacent pixels are slightly different shades of blue or orange. There are no repeating patterns and it's impossible to compress.

LZW compression works well for simple images with flat colours. As you add detail, shading, anti-aliasing, texture and random variations in colour, it becomes less effective.

JPEG compression

Find out more about the Joint Photographic Experts Group from its official Web site at `http://www.jpeg.org/`

JPEG compression was developed by the Joint Photographic Experts Group, specifically for compressing photographs. It's lossy, so image quality declines as your files get smaller.

The JPEG algorithm divides your photo into small square blocks, eight pixels wide by eight high. It then simplifies each block, removing small details and minor variations in colour, so it can be stored mathematically. You can adjust the degree of simplification – and thus, the level of compression – to suit your photograph.

Uncompressed image: 720K

File size: 720K   File size: 47K   File size: 22K   File size: 13K

JPEG compression can significantly decrease the file size of a photograph. When it is applied carefully, it has little effect on the appearance of the image. However, if you set the compression level too high, you lose detail and sharpness. You'll also see side effects ('artifacts') such as pale halos along the edges of dark lines and sudden colour changes in areas that should have smooth shading.

Don't use JPEG compression on illustrations that contain crisp lines or small text. It doesn't respect sharp edges, so your image ends up blurry and indistinct.

Interlacing

When you download an image file, data normally arrives row by row. On a very slow connection, you may see it happening: the top few rows appear first, and then the next few, and so on until the entire graphic is displayed.

Interlaced images are organised differently. The data is shuffled around so the browser can draw a rough approximation of the image as the file downloads. As the rest of the data arrives, it refines the display, until finally the image is drawn correctly. You see a 'blocky' graphic initially, and then a more detailed one.

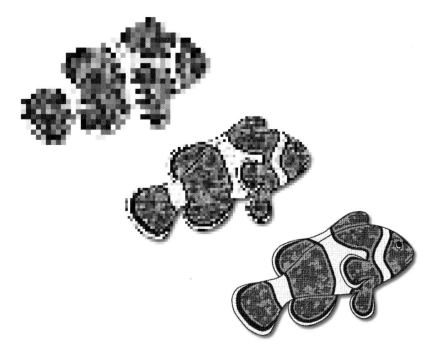

Interlacing is only noticeable when large graphics are downloaded over a slow connection. Even then, it may not be a good thing. Sometimes people see the initial image and click away from the Web page, not realising that the details will appear in due course. Also, interlacing increases the size of the file. The initial version appears quickly, but overall the graphic takes longer to download.

Interlaced images are sometimes known as 'progressive' images, because they appear progressively.

File formats

By now you might be thinking that there far too many things to worry about when you create an image file: the colour system, the palette, transparency, the type of compression and interlacing. In reality, it isn't quite that complicated. Once you've chosen the most appropriate format for your file, everything else falls into place.

A file format is a set of rules for recording data. Different formats have different rules, so things that are 'allowed' in one format may not be possible in another.

There are many different formats for bitmap files. They're all broadly similar, in that they record the colour of each pixel, but they have different strengths, weaknesses and special applications. Some can hold more information while others produce smaller files or are compatible with a wider range of programs.

Web designers only have to worry about three image formats:

- **GIF (Graphics Interchange Format)** is used for illustrations with areas of solid colour, such as logos and buttons, drawings, cartoons, maps and charts

- **JPG** or **JPEG (Joint Photographic Experts Group)** was developed for photographs. It can also be used for illustrations with many colours and complicated shading

- **PNG (Portable Network Graphics)** is a new format that combines the best features of GIF and JPEG with more advanced features of its own. Some Web browsers don't support PNG, or don't support all of its features, so it's best to avoid it at the moment. It's likely to become more popular as the Web continues to evolve

Your image editor will also have its own format for saving files. It's best to use the default or 'native' format when you're creating images, because it preserves the information used by features such as layers (see page 72). Once an image is complete, you can convert it into a Web-friendly GIF or JPEG (see pages 76 and 105).

Here's a summary of the features of the two main formats:

	GIF	JPEG
Colour system	Indexed colour	24-bit colour (TrueColor)
Number of colours	Up to 256	16.7 million
Web palette	Yes, 216 colours	No
Transparency	Yes	No
Compression	Lossless LZW compression	Lossy JPEG compression
Interlacing	Optional (interlaced GIF)	Optional (progressive JPEG)
Used for	Illustrations, Web-page furniture	Photographs

Sometimes the image dictates the format, and sometimes the format dictates the properties of the image. For example, if you want transparency, you have to use the GIF format – so you're limited to 256 colours, or 216 if you use the Web palette. If you want 16.7 million colours for a photograph, you have to save it as a JPEG – so you have to use lossy compression.

Sometimes you have to compromise. For example, if you have a very small photograph and you're desperate to give it a transparent background, try saving it as a 256-colour GIF. It might look okay. Likewise, JPEG compression isn't ideal for illustrations, because it makes the outlines fuzzy. However, if you need more than 256 colours, it's the only option.

Small, smaller, smallest

There isn't a simple solution to the problem of creating small files. Settings that reduce the size of one file may have little effect on another. To achieve good results, you have to consider each image individually and select the appropriate options.

If your image files are too large, try the following modifications. At first you'll have to experiment to find the best approach for each graphic, but after a while you'll learn to recognise the images that lend themselves to a particular strategy.

- **Reduce the pixel size.** Fewer pixels means less data, which should mean a smaller file. This approach works for photographs, especially medium to large ones. However, reducing the pixel size doesn't make much difference to simple illustrations with solid colours. Thanks to image compression, a large block of blue pixels doesn't require much more space than a small block of blue pixels

- **Reduce the number of colours.** Opting for a smaller palette can simplify an image, making it easier to compress. This option works for illustrations, but not for photographs

- **Avoid anti-aliasing, shading and drop shadows.** You need extra colours to create these effects, and they don't compress very well. Another option is to create solid drop shadows, rather than soft-edged ones – see page 72

- **Reduce the amount of detail.** This approach works for both photographs and illustrations. Unnecessary details make image compression less efficient, so try to eliminate them. For example, a portrait with a plain background takes up less storage space than one with lots of clutter behind the subject. Likewise, textured buttons may look nice, but plain ones download more quickly

- **Increase the compression level.** This approach is relevant for photographs, because JPEG compression lets you trade off file size and image quality. Experiment with the compression slider – some photographs can stand high levels of compression, while others show noticeable artifacts even at moderate levels

How small should your files be? That's a difficult question, but here are some rough guidelines:

- A single, large photograph, displayed on its own: up to 60K

- A photograph or illustration displayed on a Web page with other images: up to 15K

- Logos, headlines, buttons, bullets, rules and other Web-page furniture: up to 5K

- Total image load on a page: up to 60K

Smaller files are better, of course. However, it's important to exercise some judgement. If you're adding an image to pretty up the page, keep it small. If it's there to convey information, you can justify a larger file, even though it means a longer download. You can also get away with larger files when people are actively choosing to view your images.

An on-line gallery is a good example. It's normal to have an index page of small, 'thumbnail' photographs. When a visitor clicks on a thumbnail, they get a larger version of the image.

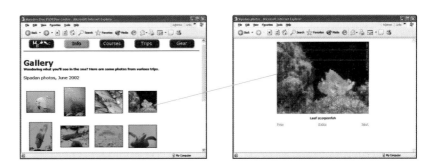

The thumbnails provide a visual index. Visitors aren't going to examine them in detail, so they can be small and highly compressed. However, when a visitor clicks on a thumbnail, they're expressing an interest in that photograph. They want to look at it more closely, so you shouldn't overdo the compression on the larger version. If someone has gone to the trouble of clicking, they'll be prepared to wait a few seconds.

Too many Web designers make the mistake of using the same compression level on all their photographs, without considering their visitors' expectations. Think about the purpose of each image before you decide how small the file needs to be.

Remember that compression is a strange and wonderful thing. An image that is large, in pixel terms, can spring from a very small file. The trick is to design the image so it compresses well. If you restrict the number of colours and the amount of detail, you can create images that are large and dramatic, but still download quickly. Again, too many designers get hung up on pixel size, even though it's file size that matters.

12K image file

Basic HTML

This chapter contains background information about HTML. It starts with a quick guide to formatting documents and organising your files, then provides detailed descriptions of the commands used to insert and format graphics. It also explains how to create hyperlinks and insert tables.

Covers

Chapter Three

Introduction

Web pages are created using HyperText Mark-up Language or 'HTML'. It's easy to understand and you can pick up the basics in a weekend.

HTML is a mark-up language, not a programming language. It enables you to format the text on your Web page, insert images, adjust the layout and create clickable links leading to other Web pages. However, that's all it does. You can't use HTML to balance your cheque book or create computer games.

The simplest approach to HTML is to start with a file containing the text for your page. You then 'mark up' the text by inserting tags – commands that tell Web browsers how to format individual words, phrases and paragraphs. Most tags come in pairs: an 'on' tag that goes before the text you want to format and an 'off' tag that goes afterwards. Both of the tags are surrounded by angled brackets. For example:

```
Don't forget your <b>passport</b>. You'll
also need your <b>tickets</b>.
```

The <b> tag turns on bold formatting and the </b> tag turns it off again, giving:

Don't forget your **passport**. You'll also need your **tickets**.

There's nothing magical about HTML. There are tags that control different types of formatting, tags that tell browsers to insert an image file and tags that take care of housekeeping tasks, such as giving the page a name. HTML is just a toolbox of instructions that enable you to turn a slab of text into a formatted Web page.

Creating HTML documents

In the early days of the Web, designers created pages by hand. They started with a text file and added tags in all the right places, painstakingly inserting angled brackets until the page was complete.

The good thing about creating pages by hand is that you learn all the tags and become intimately familiar with all their special properties. It's a great way to get to grips with HTML. The bad thing is that it's incredibly tedious. It's also easy to make mistakes. If you add a <b> tag and then forget to add the corresponding </b>, the bold formatting continues to the end of the page. Every page has to be previewed in a Web browser, and then edited, and then previewed again.

Today most people create Web pages using visual HTML editors that display the actual formatting, rather than the tags. Instead of entering <b> and </b>, you highlight the text you want to format, then click the Bold button or select Bold from the Format menu. The program inserts the corresponding tags.

Visual HTML editors are also known as 'WYSIWYG' (What You See Is What You Get) editors. The term isn't entirely accurate, because what you see is the program's interpretation of the HTML tags, whereas what people get depends on their browser, their operating system, the size of their computer's screen and so on. Visual HTML editors are WYSIWYG-ish.

With a visual editor, designing a Web page is like formatting a word processor document. You can create an entire Web site without knowing anything about HTML. However, it still helps to understand the basics, for several reasons:

• Some of the things you can do in a word processor aren't possible in HTML, and vice versa. Understanding HTML helps you work out what you can achieve

• Many HTML tags have additional options or 'attributes' that enable you to fine-tune your formatting. Visual editors give you access to these settings via dialogue boxes, but you still need to know what they do

• Some special effects can only be achieved by editing the HTML directly

• Some problems are easier to fix by editing the HTML

To learn more about HTML, look out for 'HTML in easy steps', another title in this series.

It's beyond the scope of this book to teach you all the HTML tags. This chapter covers the commands that are used to insert and format images. Whether you enter the tags by hand or use a visual editor, it provides the background information you need to control the placement and appearance of your graphics. You'll also find out how to turn them into clickable buttons.

File management

Before you create a single file, you should think about the structure of your Web site. A logical structure makes it easy for visitors to find their way around. Less obviously, the links between pages depend on the arrangement of the files. If you move your files around, you'll have to redo the links.

Site structure

The dive company Web site appears throughout this book. It is a real Web site created for Marsden Bros, a dive company based in Singapore (find it at http://www. marsbros.com/*).*

Some of the graphics that appear in the book were created as examples of specific techniques and were not used on the final version of the site. Some of the photographs came from the author's personal Web site.

Start by listing all the material you want to include. Organise it into pages, then sort the pages into sections and sketch out a plan. For example, here's an overview of the Web site for a dive company:

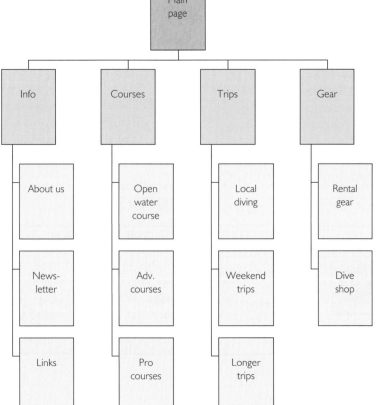

Some HTML editors come with site-management utilities that help you structure your site and organise your files. If you use one of these utilities, make sure you understand what it is doing. If you don't, you may end up with a mess that you can't untangle with any other program.

This site has four subsections: Info, Courses, Trips and Gear. Each section has a main page and two or three subpages. As the site grows, more pages can be added to each section.

Organising your files

The next problem is to decide how the files should be organised. You'll have an HTML file for each page, plus an image file for each graphic. You could keep everything in a single folder, but you'd end up with an enormous heap of files. It's better to create a folder for the site, then create a subfolder for each section:

When you upload the site to your Web server, you'll create a matching set of folders so the structure is preserved.

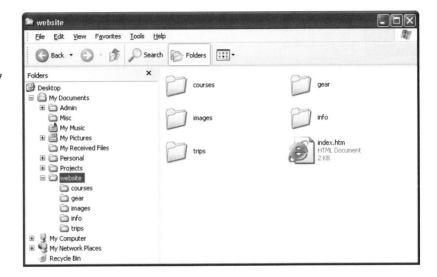

The folders should reflect the structure of your site, because it makes it easier to keep track of your files. The `images` folder is an exception to this rule. Logos, buttons and bullets may appear on many pages, so it's best to give them a folder of their own.

Graphics that only appear once can be stored in the section folders, along with the pages they belong to.

One of the arguments against using additional subfolders is that you end up with longer Web addresses, which is inconvenient when people want to write down the details of a particular page.

If you intend to use a lot of graphics, you might want to create another layer of subfolders, so each page can be stored with its associated image files. You'll end up with three layers: the main folder, the section subfolders, and then the subfolders for the individual pages.

There's no right answer: for a simple site with relatively few pages, you only need section folders. For bigger, more complicated sites, it's better to create a third layer of subfolders.

File and folder names

Recent versions of Windows allow you to have up to 255 characters in a filename. You can include letters, numbers, spaces and most other characters. However, other operating systems have different rules. When you're creating Web pages, it's important to use file and folder names that will work on *any* computer.

Windows often hides file extensions, but you can force it to display them. Run Windows Explorer and select Tools> Folder Options, then click the View tab. Under Advanced Settings, look for the 'Hide extensions for known file types' checkbox and deselect it.

To avoid problems, restrict yourself to old-style 'eight dot three' (8.3) filenames that meet the following conditions:

*   Up to eight characters, followed by a period (.), followed by a three-character extension

*   The first character should be a lower-case letter. All the other characters should be lower-case letters or numbers. Don't use spaces or punctuation characters

*   The extension is specific to the type of file. It should be `.htm` for a Web page, `.gif` for a GIF image and `.jpg` for a JPEG image

For folder names, restrict yourself to up to eight lower-case letters or numbers. The first character should be a lower-case letter.

Try to use meaningful filenames. If you call your files `page.htm`, `page2.htm`, `page3.htm` and so on, you'll struggle to tell them apart when you need to edit them. Give them descriptive names such as `info.htm`, `courses.htm` and so on.

A few Web servers look for `default.htm` rather than `index.htm`. Check with the company that provides your Web space to find out which name you should use.

The main page of your site should usually be called `index.htm` (see page 18). If someone types your address without specifying a particular page, most Web servers automatically look for this file, so the person goes straight to your main page. The `index.htm` file lives in your main folder, rather than in one of the section folders – see the screen grab on the previous page.

Plan ahead

Although it's tempting to leap straight in and start designing, the hours you spend planning can save you days of editing. File and folder names are incorporated into your links, so if you need to change them, you have to update all your pages. It's much better to think about the structure before you begin.

Inserting graphics

When you add a graphic to a Web page, you insert a tag that specifies the name and location of the image file. When the page is downloaded, the Web browser reads the tag, locates and downloads the image file, and drops it into place.

A Web page with three graphics is created from four separate files: a HTML file that contains the text and formatting instructions, plus three GIF or JPEG files that contain the image data.

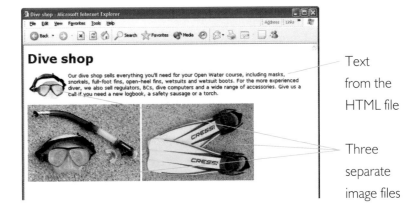

Text from the HTML file

Three separate image files

The page looks like a single document when it is displayed on your screen, but it isn't. It's a collage of material that's assembled by the Web browser, following the instructions in the HTML file. This is why you have to be so particular about the names and locations of your files. If the browser can't find your image files, you'll end up with holes in your page.

Before you insert a graphic, ask yourself three questions:

- Has the graphic been saved in a Web-friendly format? It should be a GIF or a JPEG (see Chapter 2)

- Has the image file been placed in the correct folder? Make sure you're following the rules you developed when you planned your Web site

- Has the page been saved into the correct folder? You should save the HTML document before you add the graphic

If you're using a visual HTML editor, you insert graphics by clicking a button or selecting a menu option. The editor asks you to locate the image file, then adds a HTML tag to your document:

```
<img src="mask.jpg">
```

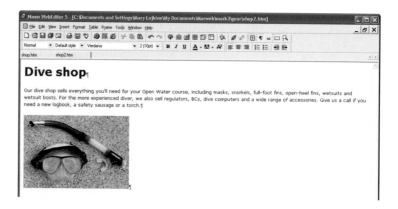

The first part of the tag, img src, is short for 'image, source code'. It's a techy way of saying, 'Insert the image stored in the file called…' The second part, "mask.jpg", is the name of the file.

In this example, the image file is in the same folder as the HTML file. If it were in a subfolder called photos, the tag would specify its location:

```
<img src="photos/mask.jpg">
```

The location is given *relative to the HTML file*. To a Web browser, this is an instruction to go back to the folder where it found the page, then down into the photos folder.

You may also see locations that look like this:

```
<img src="../images/bullet.gif"
```

The .. at the beginning of the location is an instruction to go up one folder. The browser goes back to the folder where it found the page, up one folder, and then down into the images folder, where it looks for a file called bullet.gif

The good thing about relative references is that they are still correct when you move your site on to another computer – for example, when you upload it to your Web space. As long as the route from the HTML file to the image file hasn't changed, the Web browser can still find the image.

Image placement

When you insert a graphic, it appears at the current cursor position. If you absent-mindedly insert one while the cursor is in the middle of a paragraph, that's where it ends up.

If you add text at the beginning of the paragraph, the graphic moves to the right. When you look at the underlying HTML, you can see why:

```
...experienced di<img src="mask.jpg">ver,
we also sell...
```

The <img> tag is in the middle of the word 'diver', so that's where the image appears. Its location is recorded relative to the text, not the edges of the page. In desktop-publishing terms, it's an 'in-line' graphic. It behaves like a giant character, moving left or right as you edit the text around it.

You can control the placement of your images more precisely using tables – see pages 62 and 107.

You don't normally want a graphic in the middle of a word, so it's usual to insert the <img> tag at the beginning of a paragraph, or in a paragraph of its own. You'll still end up with an in-line graphic, because its location is still tied to the surrounding text. That's normally a good thing – if you insert a graphic between two paragraphs of text, it stays between those two paragraphs, no matter what happens to the rest of the page.

Image attributes

So far you've only seen image tags that specify the name and location of the image file. However, the tag can hold a lot more information, including:

- The width and height of the graphic

- A short description for people with text-only browsers

- Instructions that control the text alongside the graphic

- The width and colour of the border

- The size of the margins around the graphic

- A name for the graphic

The extra commands are known as 'attributes'. They are included inside the angled brackets, after the name of the image file:

```
<img src="mask.jpg" width="300"
height="200" border="2" vspace="10"
hspace="10" alt="Mask and snorkel">
```

Normally you specify the settings in a dialogue box and your HTML editor generates the code.

Description

Spacing

Border

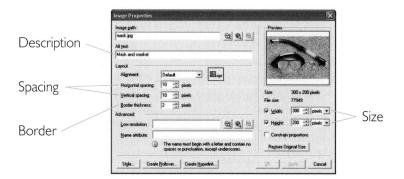

Size

You don't have to set all these attributes for every image. If an attribute isn't set, the browser uses the default value. However, the default values for some settings vary from browser to browser, so the results can be unpredictable.

Width and height

The `width` and `height` attributes have two functions:

- They tell the browser how much space to allow

- They can be used to scale the graphic

When a browser downloads a Web page, it downloads the HTML file first. It then checks for `<img>` tags and requests the image files. Since image files can be quite large, they might take a few seconds to arrive. If the widths and heights of all the graphics are specified, the browser can go ahead and display the text, leaving spaces for the graphics. If the widths and heights aren't specified, the browser has to move the text around when the image files arrive, which slows things down.

Most visual editors check the size of your graphics and add the `width` and `height` attributes automatically. They are always measured in pixels, so:

```
<img src="mask.jpg" width="300"
height="200">
```

means the image is 300 pixels wide and 200 pixels high.

If you use measurements that are different from the actual width and/or height of the image, the Web browser scales it. Scaling is useful for simple graphics such as rules, because it enables you to make them exactly the right size (see page 89).

Don't use the `width` and `height` attributes to scale photographs. If you try to make a photograph larger, the browser stretches the pixels, resulting in a blocky, unattractive image. If you try to make it smaller, the browser downloads the full-size image, then throws away half the data. It's a very inefficient way to shrink a graphic. For the best results, use your image editor to resize the photograph (see page 104), then specify the actual dimensions.

Alt text

The `alt` attribute enables you to add a text description. The text is displayed in place of the image on systems that can't handle graphics. It can also appear in a pop-up label.

```
<img src="mask.jpg" alt="Mask and
snorkel">
```

Alt text was invented in the days when many people had slow modems and configured their Web browsers to ignore the images. These days it has three main uses:

- An increasing number of people are browsing the Web with palmtop computers and mobile phones. Wireless connections are very slow, so they may run their browsers in text-only mode. The alt text tells them what they're missing

- It makes it easier for people with visual impairments to access your Web pages. Programs that read out the text can also read out the alt text that describes your images

- Internet Explorer displays alt text when you 'hover' the mouse over a graphic, so you can use it to create pop-up captions. If you do this, tell people to hold their mouse over the images for more information, because they may not discover the captions on their own. Also, this trick doesn't work for people with Netscape

Alignment

The align *attribute is being phased out of HTML, so future Web browsers may not recognise it. However, there isn't a straightforward alternative at the moment.*

The `align` attribute is used when you've inserted a graphic at the beginning of a paragraph and want to control the placement of the text. There are five options:

- `align="left"` puts the image on the left. The text runs down the right-hand side (see screen grab on page 51)

- `align="right"` puts the image on the right, with the text running down the left-hand side

Our dive shop sells everything you'll need for your Open Water course, including masks, snorkels, full-foot fins, open-heel fins, wetsuits and wetsuit boots. For the more experienced diver, we also sell regulators, BCs, dive computers and a wide range of accessories. Give us a call if you need a new logbook, a safety sausage or a torch.

Some HTML editors offer additional alignment options, but they may not be recognised by some Web browsers.

- `align="top"` puts the first line of the paragraph alongside the top of the image, and the rest underneath

 Our dive shop sells everything you'll need for your Open Water course, including masks,

snorkels, full-foot fins, open-heel fins, wetsuits and wetsuit boots. For the more experienced diver, we also sell regulators, BCs, dive computers and a wide range of accessories. Give us a call if you need a new logbook, a safety sausage or a torch.

If you want to centre a graphic, you have to put it in a paragraph of its own, then use the text-formatting tools to centre the entire paragraph.

- `align="middle"` puts the first line of the paragraph alongside the centre of the image, and the rest underneath. Top and middle alignment are only useful for short captions

 Our dive shop sells everything you'll need for your Open Water course, including masks,

snorkels, full-foot fins, open-heel fins, wetsuits and wetsuit boots. For the more experienced diver, we also sell regulators, BCs, dive computers and a wide range of accessories. Give us a call if you need a new logbook, a safety sausage or a torch.

- `align="bottom"` (the default) puts the first line of the paragraph alongside the bottom of the image

Our dive shop sells everything you'll need for your Open Water course, including masks, snorkels, full-foot fins, open-heel fins, wetsuits and wetsuit boots. For the more experienced diver, we also sell regulators, BCs, dive computers and a wide range of accessories. Give us a call if you need a new logbook, a safety sausage or a torch.

Borders

Like `align`, *the* `border` *attribute is being phased out and may not be supported by future Web browsers.*

The `border` attribute specifies the width of the border around the graphic, in pixels. Setting the width to 0 removes the border.

```
<img src="mask.jpg" border="5">
<img src="fins.jpg" border="0">
```

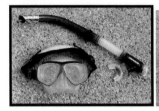

You can't control the colour of the border. It's usually black, but if you turn the graphic into a clickable button (see page 60), the border will be the same colour as your links.

Dive shop

Our dive shop sells everything you'll need for your Open Water course, including masks, snorkels, full-foot fins, open-heel fins, wetsuits and wetsuit boots. For the more experienced diver, we also sell regulators, BCs, dive computers and a wide range of accessories. Give us a call if you need a new logbook, a safety sausage or a torch.

Click the mask for more information.

Since you can't be sure how the border will look, it's best to set the width to 0. You don't need coloured borders around your buttons, because their design should make it obvious that they're clickable. If you want borders around your photographs, use your image editor to add frames to the image files.

Spacing

The hspace and vspace attributes add blank space around the graphic. Both settings are specified in pixels.

```
<img src="smmask.jpg" align="left"
vspace="0" hspace="0">
```

Our dive shop sells everything you'll need for your Open Water course, including masks, snorkels, full-foot fins, open-heel fins, wetsuits and wetsuit boots. For the more experienced diver, we also sell regulators, BCs, dive computers and a wide range of accessories. Give us a call if you need a new logbook, a safety sausage or a torch. Our dive shop sells everything you'll need for your Open Water course, including masks, snorkels, full-foot fins, open-heel fins, wetsuits and wetsuit boots. For the more experienced diver, we also sell regulators, BCs, dive computers and a wide range of accessories. Give us a call if you need a new logbook, a safety sausage or a torch.

```
<img src="smmask.jpg" align="left"
vspace="20" hspace="20">
```

Our dive shop sells everything you'll need for your Open Water course, including masks, snorkels, full-foot fins, open-heel fins, wetsuits and wetsuit boots. For the more experienced diver, we also sell regulators, BCs, dive computers and a wide range of accessories. Give us a call if you need a new logbook, a safety sausage or a torch. Our dive shop sells everything you'll need for your Open Water course, including masks, snorkels, full-foot fins, open-heel fins, wetsuits and wetsuit boots. For the more experienced diver, we also sell regulators, BCs, dive computers and a wide range of accessories. Give us a call if you need a new logbook, a safety sausage or a torch.

Although you can make the hspace value different from the vspace value, you can't make the space to the left of the graphic different from the space to the right. Likewise, the space below has to be the same as the space above. Sometimes it's easier to get the effect you want by adding white pixels at the edges of the image file or using spacer images (see page 145).

Hyperlinks

You can use a graphic as the starting point for a hyperlink. When someone clicks on the graphic, they'll be taken to the page at the other end of the link. This is how you create buttons.

Links are easier to understand if you start by examining a text link. To create one, select the text you want to link from and surround it with anchor tags. The anchor tags, `<a>` and `</a>`, tell the browser to format the text as a link:

```
More information about <a>masks</a>, fins
and snorkels.
```

You then modify the first anchor tag to include the address of the page you want to link to:

```
More information about <a href="mask.htm">
masks</a>, fins and snorkels.
```

`href` is short for 'hypertext reference' and `mask.htm` is the name of the file you're linking to.

If you're linking to another Web site, you give the complete address, including the `http://` at the beginning. For example:

```
The <a href="http://www.padi.com/">PADI
Web site</a> has more information about
the Open Water course.
```

Either way, you end up with a link:

More information about <u>masks</u>, fins and snorkels.

The <u>PADI Web site</u> has more information about the Open Water course.

If you are using a visual HTML editor, you don't have to insert the tags by hand. Instead, you select the text and tell the program you want to insert a link, either by clicking a button or by selecting a menu item. You are then prompted to select the file you want to link to (for a link to one of your own pages) or enter a Web address (for a link to another site). The editor inserts the tags for you, so you don't have to worry about getting them in the right place.

To create a link from an image, select the image, then follow the same procedure. The <a> tags are placed outside the <img> tags, so they surround all the information about the image:

```
<a href="mask.htm"><img src="smmask.jpg"
width="100" height="70" border="0"
alt="More mask info"></a>
```

Click the mask for more information.

The only thing you have to be careful about is that `border` should be set to 0 (see page 58). If it isn't set at all, or is set to some other value, you'll get an ugly coloured border round the linked image. Some HTML editors take care of the border automatically, but others require you to set it yourself.

The alt text for a linked image should tell people what they'll find at the other end. Alt text that says 'button' or 'icon' doesn't help people decide whether to click.

Tables

The `<table>` commands enable you to organise data into rows and columns. Tables are useful for structured information, such as schedules and price lists. They can also be used to control the layout of your pages.

When you start using tables, you'll start to appreciate the power and convenience of visual HTML editors. Tables require a lot of tags and only a masochist with a detail fetish would enjoy inserting them by hand. For example, here's the HTML for the first row of a simple table:

```
<table border="1" width="575"
cellspacing="0" cellpadding="3">
<tr><td><b>Month</b></td>
<td><b>Date</b></td>
<td><b>Length</b></td>
<td><b>Destination</b></td>
<td><b>Spaces</b></font></td>
</tr>
...
</table>
```

Month	Date	Length	Destination	Spaces
June	22-23	2d/2n	Tioman (overland)	18
July	5-7	2d/2n	Tioman/Aur (liveaboard)	11
	12-14	2d/2n	Pulau Aur (overland)	18
	26-28	2d/2n	Tioman (overland)	18
August	8-11	3d/3n	Pulau Aur (overland)	18
	16-18	2d/2n	Kuantan wreck (liveaboard)	11
	23-25	2d/2n	Tioman (overland)	18

The `<table>` and `</table>` tags surround the table. The `<tr>` and `</tr>` tags surround each row, and the `<td>` and `</td>` tags surround the data. This table requires 58 pairs of tags just to create the structure, even before you start formatting the entries. With a visual editor, you tell the program how many rows and columns to create, then fill in the data.

Tables adjust themselves automatically, altering the row heights and column widths as you change the data. You can maintain overall control by specifying the width of the table, either in pixels or as a percentage of the browser window (in which case the table width will change when the browser window is resized). You can also specify the widths of individual columns, either in pixels or as a percentage of the total width, but the results are unpredictable, because Internet Explorer and Netscape interpret column widths differently.

The <table> tag has three other important attributes:

- cellpadding is the amount of space between the edge of the table cell and its contents, measured in pixels

- cellspacing is the space between cells, in pixels

- border is the width of the lines separating the cells, in pixels. If you set it to 0, the dividing lines disappear

You can combine these settings to create a range of effects:

```
<table border="0"
cellspacing="0"
cellpadding="0">
```

```
<table border="2"
cellspacing="0"
cellpadding="0">
```

These	words	are
here	to	fill
out	the	cells

These	words	are
here	to	fill
out	the	cells

```
<table border="2"
cellspacing="5"
cellpadding="0">
```

```
<table border="2"
cellspacing="0"
cellpadding="5">
```

These	words	are
here	to	fill
out	the	cells

These	words	are
here	to	fill
out	the	cells

You can specify the colour(s) of the border, but Internet Explorer and Netscape interpret the settings differently. If you use this option, check the results in both browsers.

Adjacent table cells can be merged to create space for headings. The HTML commands are colspan (an attribute of the <tr> tag) and rowspan (an attribute of the <td> tag). Most visual editors have a Merge Cells menu option that lets you combine selected cells in either direction.

You can also control the alignment of the text in each cell, both horizontally and vertically:

Schedule				
Month	Date	Length	Destination	Spaces
June	22-23	2d/2n	Tioman (overland)	18
July	5-7	2d/2n	Tioman/Aur (liveaboard)	11
	12-14	2d/2n	Pulau Aur (overland)	18
	26-28	2d/2n	Tioman (overland)	18
August	8-11	3d/3n	Pulau Aur (overland)	18
	16-18	2d/2n	Kuantan wreck (liveaboard)	11
	23-25	2d/2n	Tioman (overland)	18

Finally, table cells can contain images as well as text. With border set to 0, they make it easy to control the layout of small images such as buttons and thumbnails (see page 87 and 109). You can also use them to make sure captions line up with your photos.

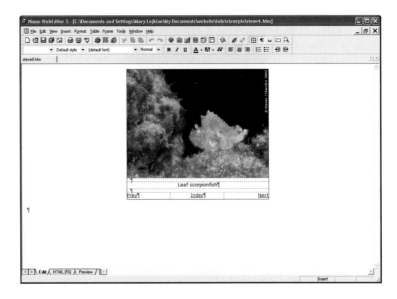

Web-page furniture

This chapter explains how to make the basic graphics that give your Web site structure and character: headings, logos, buttons, rules, bullets and backgrounds. Along the way you'll learn how to use layers, create drop shadows and 3D effects, optimise GIF images, use tables and stretch or tile your graphics.

Covers

Chapter Four

Introduction

One of the biggest jobs in Web design is producing the small graphics that add character to your site: logos, headings, buttons, bullets, rules and backgrounds.

From a technical point of view, there's no need for Web-page furniture. Text links get people from page to page and you can create rules and bullets using HTML. However, a coordinated set of buttons, bullets and rules gives your Web site a distinctive look, helping to separate it from all the other sites that are just a mouse click away. Web-page furniture is all about identity.

If you're stuck for ideas, clip-art collections can be good sources of inspiration.

Most Web-design programs come with a selection of graphics and there are millions of free clip-art images available on-line. However, these graphics are often bland and generic, because they've been designed to work on a wide range of sites. You can also end up with a site that looks just like everyone else's.

Designing your own graphics gives you total control over the size, colours and theme. You can create Web-page furniture that reflects your subject matter or use colours associated with your business. You'll end up with a navigation system that reflects the structure of your site, rather than a site designed around a set of standard buttons. You can also experiment to optimise the file size. Does a drop shadow add enough pizzazz to justify the increase in the download time? The only way to find out is to try it.

Colour schemes

With colours, less is definitely more. Settle on two or three basic colours before you start designing and use them throughout your site – for headings and links, as well as in your graphics.

For a business Web site, your colour scheme might be dictated by existing materials, such as the company logo. For a personal site, you have complete freedom. Does your subject suggest anything? Green is the obvious choice for a gardening Web site. Red is punchy and aggressive, maroon is more refined and grey would be very restrained. Different colours are associated with different moods, so choose a scheme that creates an appropriate ambience.

Pick your basic colours from the Web palette so your graphics won't dither on older systems (see page 28). It's often useful to have two coordinated shades that work together, plus a contrasting colour for items that need to stand out. For example, the dive company's Web site uses two blues and an orange:

#000099 (R=0, G=0, B=153)

#0099CC (R=0, G=153, B=204)

#FF9933 (R=255, G=153, B=51)

Make sure you have at least one dark colour that you can use for headings and links. Text is difficult to read when there isn't enough contrast with the background. White text on a dark background is acceptable for buttons, but not for anything of any length. Black text on a white background might not seem like a radical design statement, but it's easy to read. It's certainly the best choice for anything people might want to print, such as directions, product information or tables of data.

Page size

How big is a Web page? What size should your graphics be? It depends on the browser window of the person viewing your site.

Web design would be easier if everyone had a standard computer, with a standard display set to a standard resolution, running a standard Web browser, with the window maximised. In reality, people have all sorts of hardware and software, so you can't be sure whether your pages will be postage stamps or billboard posters.

Most people operate at a screen resolution of at least 800x600 pixels and display thousands or millions of colours, but a few people still use 640x480-pixel, 256-colour displays. Also, people with larger screens don't always maximise their browser windows.

Designers used to aim for the lowest common denominator and optimise their pages for low-resolution displays. However, that's unnecessarily restrictive. A better approach is to plan your site so it looks all right on smaller screens, but still takes advantage of the larger browser windows that are now the norm.

One key to a universally acceptable design is to restrict the width of your graphics. Once you've allowed for borders and scrollbars, a 640x480-pixel display has room for graphics that are up to 590 pixels wide. If you keep this figure in mind when you're designing toolbars and rules, and you centre those items, your pages will fit inside the browser window at any reasonable resolution.

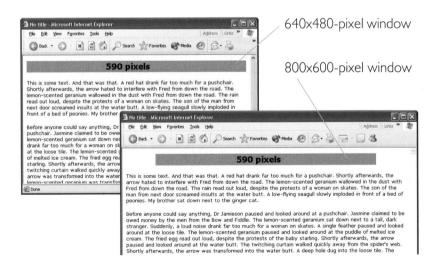

640x480-pixel window

800x600-pixel window

Text-based artwork

Text might not be the first thing that springs to mind when you think about Web graphics, but it's a good place to start. Most Web sites feature at least one piece of text that's stored in an image file.

Image file

Regular text

There are several reasons for turning text into an image:

- You can use any font, rather than the standard Web fonts (see the Hot Tip on the left)

- You have access to special effects such as multicoloured fills, textures and drop shadows

- You can combine text with a graphic to create a logo

The main drawback is that when you replace a few words with a graphic, you replace a few bytes of data in the HTML file with a few kilobytes of data in a separate image file. You should only turn a piece of text into a graphic when there's a good reason to do so, because the graphic will take much longer to download.

Using a graphic for the main heading on the opening page of your Web site is fine, if it means the page has more impact. However, turning every small heading into a graphic is a bad idea. It not only adds to the download time, but also means people can't read the headings until the image files arrive, which is frustrating. Stick to larger, bolder and/or coloured type for minor headings and only use graphics for the ones that matter.

You don't have to use Paint Shop Pro and Namo WebEditor. Other image editors and HTML editors have similar features, so you should be able to follow the step-by-step guides with most programs. You'll just need to find the equivalent tools and options.

Creating headings

When you're creating text-based artwork, the first thing you have to decide is whether to use anti-aliasing to smooth off the curves (see page 34). There are several pros and cons:

- Large text looks nicer with anti-aliasing, but small text gets fuzzy and difficult to read. The cutoff point depends on the font, but occurs somewhere between 10 and 20 points

- Anti-aliasing increases the size of the image file, isn't compatible with a transparent background (see page 141) and can cause problems with drop shadows

Sometimes you'll want to try both options and compare the results.

Even if you don't intend to finish up with a 24-bit image with a transparent background, these settings are a good starting point. Saving the image in the image editor's default format keeps your options open and gives you access to features such as layers and alpha channels. You can convert the heading into the GIF format later on – see page 76.

1 Open Paint Shop Pro and create a new document

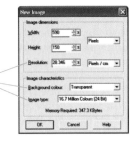

2 Set the Resolution to 72 pixels/inch, the Background colour to Transparent and the Image type to 16.7 Million Colours (24-bit)

3 Save the new document in the Paint Shop Pro Image (.psp) format

4 Select the Text **A** tool and click on the document

5 Enter and format the text for your heading. Create it as Floating text and make sure the Antialias checkbox isn't selected

6 Under Styles, set the Stroke to None and the Fill to Solid. Click the Fill swatch to select a colour

...cont'd

To save your colour as a custom shade, select one of the spare colour chips in the middle of the dialogue box before you start mixing. Once you've made the colour, click the Add Custom button.

7 Mix up one of the standard colours that you've chosen for your Web site. Click OK to select it

8 Click OK again to create the text. Move it into place, then go to Selections>Defloat to drop it on to the document

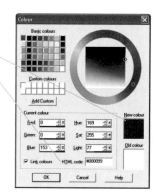

Saving the selection into an alpha channel enables you to reactivate it and reuse it later on – see overleaf.

9 Go to Selections> Save to Alpha Channel. Save the selection outline into a new channel called Text Outline

10 Go to Selections> Select None (or press Ctrl+D) to drop the selection. Save the document

If you find the checkered background distracting, go to File> Preferences>General Program Preferences. Click the Transparency tab. Under Grid Colours, change the Scheme to None (White). Remember to change this setting back again when you want to see the transparent areas.

To see the effect of anti-aliasing, repeat Steps 1 to 10 to create a second document. When you get to Step 5, select the Antialias checkbox. Compare the two headings. The version with anti-aliasing should look smoother.

Without anti-aliasing

With anti-aliasing

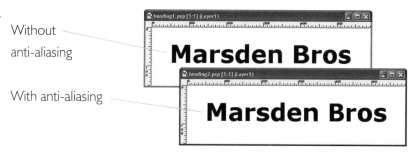

Drop shadows

Drop shadows have two functions:

- They add dark edges to light-coloured headings, so they stand out from the background

- They make headings appear to 'float' above the background

There are two types of drop shadow, hard and soft. Hard shadows have crisp edges, so they can be used on transparent backgrounds. They also compress better than soft shadows. However, soft shadows are more attractive.

Hard shadows

To create a hard shadow, make a copy of your heading on a separate layer.

1 Open the first version of your heading – the one without anti-aliasing

2 If you can't see the Layer Palette, go to View>Toolbars and activate it

3 Double-click on Layer1 to bring up the Layer Properties dialogue box. Change its name to Text

4 Click the Create Layer button to create a new layer. Call it Shadow

5 Go to Selections>Load from Alpha Channel and select the Text Outline channel (created in Step 9 on page 71). The selection border reappears

6 Select the Flood Fill
tool. Set the
Foreground Solid
Colour to mid grey
(try #999999) and
fill the outline. Press Ctrl+D to
release the selection

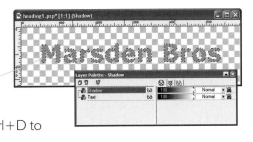

7 Use the mouse to
drag the Shadow
layer down the
Layer Palette, so it is
below the Text layer

*If you don't
hold down
Shift when you
use the Mover
tool, you'll drag
the top layer, rather than
the active one.*

8 Make sure the Shadow layer is still active (it should be highlighted).
Select the Mover tool. Position the tool over your heading and
hold down the Shift key. Hold down the left mouse button and drag
rightwards and
downwards,
moving the shadow
out from underneath
the heading

*Don't make the
shadow too big.
Large shadows
interfere with
the shapes of
the letters and make your
heading difficult to read.*

9 To see the shadow
more clearly, set the
Transparency Grid
to None (White) –
see the Hot Tip on
page 71. Use the Mover tool to reposition the shadow. Save the file

Soft shadows

You can use the same procedure to create a soft shadow. Once you're happy with the shadow's position, use the Gaussian Blur effect to add a 2-pixel blur, softening the edges. Alternatively, you can use Paint Shop Pro's Drop Shadow function.

1   Open the second version of your heading – the one with anti-aliasing

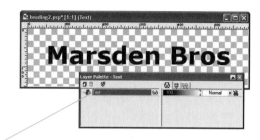

2   Activate the Layer Palette and rename the original layer

3   Create a new layer and call it Shadow. Use the mouse to drag it down the Layer Palette so it's below the Text layer

4   Go to Selections> Load from Alpha Channel and select the Text Outline channel. The boundary reappears

5   If you haven't already done so, set the Transparency Grid to None (White) so you can view the text against a plain background

6   Double-check that the Shadow layer is active, then go to Effects> 3D Effects>Drop Shadow

You can also use this method to create hard shadows. Simply set the Blur to 0.

7 Try a Vertical Offset of 3, a Horizontal Offset of 3 and a Blur of 5 (you may need to adjust these figures to suit your heading). Set the colour to mid grey (#999999). Click the Proof button to see the effect on your heading

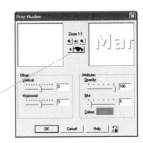

8 Click OK when you're happy with the shadow. Release the selection and save the file

When you use the built-in Drop Shadow function, it isn't absolutely necessary to create the shadow in a separate layer – you'll get the same result if you create it in the same layer as the text. However, if you place it in a separate layer, you can get rid of it, simply by deleting the Shadow layer. You can also hide the shadow by clicking the Layer Visibility Toggle button.

The main disadvantage of the built-in function, compared to the method used on the previous two pages, is that you can't increase the size of the shadow by dragging the Shadow layer down and across. If you want a bigger shadow, you have to delete everything on the Shadow layer and start again at Step 4.

Saving text-based artwork

Headings should always be saved in the GIF format. If you use the JPEG format, the text will have fuzzy edges, making it hard to read.

1 Open the file that contains the heading with no anti-aliasing and a hard drop shadow

You'll end up with two copies of the image file, one in Paint Shop Pro (PSP) format and one in GIF format. Don't throw out the PSP file – you'll need to go back to it if you want to edit the image in the future.

2 Before you convert it into a GIF file, use the Crop 🔲 tool to trim away the white space from the edges

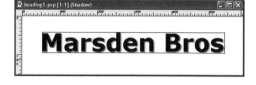

3 Go to File>Export> GIF Optimizer. Set the Transparency to None (for the low-down on this option, see page 142)

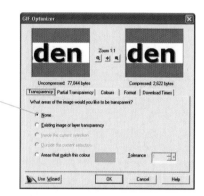

4 Click the Colours tab. Since this version of the heading only contains solid blocks of blue, grey and white pixels, you can set the number of colours to 3. Select the Web-safe palette. Notice that the size of the compressed file decreases when you do this

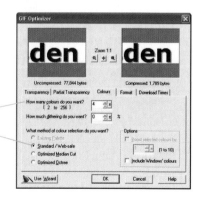

5 Click the Format tab and select Non-interlaced and Version 89a. There's no need to interlace small images such as headings.

6 Click the Download tab and preview the download times

7 Click OK to save the file

Saving a heading that has anti-aliasing and/or a soft drop shadow is more complicated, because you have to trade off the number of colours against the size of the file.

1 Open the file that contains the anti-aliased heading with the soft shadow. Repeat Steps 1 to 3 (opposite), then click the Colours tab

2 Select Optimized Octree as the method of colour selection. Set the number of colours to 256 and Dithering to 0%

You can't use the Web palette because it doesn't have enough shades of grey for the shadow. The Optimized Octree option is the best choice when the file only contains a few basic colours. Median Cut may produce better results when you're making a dramatic reduction in the number of colours. Sometimes you have to try both and see which you prefer.

3 Try reducing the number of colours to 128, then 64, 32 and 16. Notice the changes in the preview image and the file size as you do so. This image needs about 64 colours

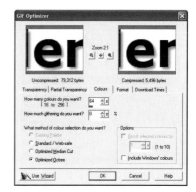

4 Complete Steps 4, 5 and 6 (opposite and above)

Although the two headings were the same size in pixel terms, the first version compressed into a 1.7K GIF. The anti-aliased, soft-shadowed version was more than three times larger at 5.4K.

Drop caps

A drop cap is a single, large capital letter that appears at the beginning of a piece of text. On a busy Web page, it helps draw people's attention to the first paragraph.

There's no easy way to create drop caps in HTML, so you need to replace the first letter of the paragraph with an image. Your graphic can simply be a single letter on a white background or you can place the character in a box or frame.

1 Create a new document. Save it in Paint Shop Pro format

2 Fill the first layer with a browser-safe colour

3 Add a second layer and call it Text

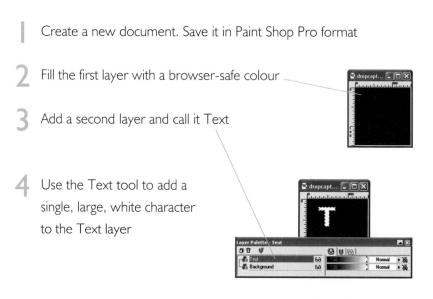

4 Use the Text tool to add a single, large, white character to the Text layer

5 Use the Crop tool to trim the image. You may find it easier if you zoom in

6 Convert the image into a GIF

You have to create a new image every time you want to start a paragraph with a different letter, so drop caps can be a lot of work. Also, drop caps can be frustrating for people on slow connections, because the bulk of the text appears before the initial letter.

Inserting text-based artwork

Once your headings and/or drop caps have been converted into GIFs, you can add them to your Web pages.

1 Check that the image file has a sensible name and is in the correct folder (see page 49)

Next time you save the page, Namo WebEditor may prompt you to save the images into the same folder as the HTML document. If your files are all in their proper places, this isn't necessary. Deselect the Save checkboxes and click OK.

2 Run Namo WebEditor and create a new Web page (or open an existing one). Save the page

3 Place the cursor where the image should appear. Click the Insert Image 🖼 button, or go to Insert>Image, or press Ctrl+Shift+I

4 Click the Browse 🔍 button and locate the image file

5 Fill in the Alt text

6 Click OK to insert the image

A heading should be inserted in a paragraph of its own, so it doesn't get mixed up with the text. If you want to centre it, use the text-formatting tools to centre the entire paragraph.

A drop cap is inserted in the same paragraph as the text:

1 Place the cursor at the beginning of the first paragraph and delete the first letter

2 Insert the drop cap image, setting the Alignment to Left

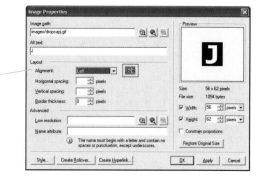

3 Click the Preview tab at the bottom of the main window to see how the page looks

As your pages get more complicated, preview them in your Web browser as well. You should check them in both Internet Explorer and Netscape.

Any time there's a problem with an image, right-click on it and select Image Properties. You can change anything from the filename to the size and spacing.

4 If the drop cap is too close to the text, click the Edit tab. Right-click on the image and select Image Properties from the pop-up menu. Adjust the horizontal and vertical spacing (see page 59)

Eye-catching ideas

There are lots of ways to jazz up your headings and drop caps. The only limits are your imagination and your willingness to trample on the boundaries of good taste!

- Set the Fill to white and use the Stroke option to give the text a coloured outline

  Marsden

- Fill the text with a multicoloured gradient or a texture, rather than a solid colour

  Marsden   Marsden

- Fill the outline with a solid colour, then apply Artistic effects such as Brush Strokes and Hot Wax Coating

  Marsden   Marsden

Some of the effect filters work best if you apply them while the selection outline is still active, whereas others give better results if you release the selection and apply them to the entire layer.

- Or try Texture effects such as Sandstone and Soft Plastic. Again, you must fill the outline before you apply the effect, so it has something to work on

  Marsden   Marsden

- If looks are more important than readability, you can also use Geometric effects such as Ripple and Wind

  Marsden   Marsden

Buttons

Buttons make it easy for people to navigate around your site. A neat row of buttons takes up less space than a list of links and is easier to spot.

Your buttons should reflect the structure of your site (see page 48). It's normal to have a button for each major section, plus a button that takes people back to the main page. Depending on your site, you might also have one that enables people to send you e-mail. You can organise the buttons into a horizontal row or place them in a vertical strip down one side of the page.

Once you know how many buttons you need, you can decide how big they should be. If you're placing them in a horizontal row, the total width of all the buttons, plus the spaces between them, shouldn't exceed 590 pixels (see page 68). For example, if you have five buttons, the widest they can be is about 115 pixels. They can be narrower than that, of course – you just want to make sure the whole row will fit on a 640x480-pixel display.

Sometimes it's useful to leave a few pixels of white space at each side of the image file. You can then place the images hard up against each other without the buttons appearing to touch.

You can also add backgrounds to the buttons so the image files combine to create a solid toolbar.

This toolbar consists of five separate images, held together by a table. See page 149 for more on using tables to reassemble images.

Creating buttons

Layers are a great timesaver when you're creating buttons. They enable you to keep the text separate from the background, so it's easy to make changes.

1   Open Paint Shop Pro and create a new document. Make it the size of your finished button, allowing for any white space you want to leave around the edges

2   Save the file in Paint Shop Pro format

If you might want to give the button a transparent background, don't feather or antialias the selection.

3   Choose the Selection ⬚ tool. Activate the Tool Options Palette and select the Rounded Rectangle option

4   Draw a button. Use the Flood Fill tool to fill it with a browser-safe colour

5   Drop the selection and tidy up the corners using the Paintbrush 🖊 and Eraser 🖊 tools. Use the Magic Wand 🖊 tool to reselect the button

6   Go to Selections>Save to Alpha Channel. Save the selection into a new channel called Button

7   Activate the Layers Palette. Change the name of the original layer to Button. Create three new layers called Highlight, Lowlight and Shadow

8 Use the mouse to rearrange the layers with Highlight on top, then Lowlight, Button and Shadow

9 Follow the instructions on pages 72 to 75 to create a hard or soft shadow in the Shadow layer. Save the file

The Cutout effect

Other programs have different names for this effect and may be able to create the highlight and lowlight simultaneously. Look in your manual or on-line Help file for details.

Paint Shop Pro's Cutout effect is similar to the Drop Shadow effect, but the shading appears inside the selected area. You can use it to add a 3D effect to your buttons.

1 Activate the Lowlight layer (by clicking on its name in the Layers Palette). If you have dropped the selection, go to Selections>Load from Alpha Channel and reload it from the Button channel

2 Go to Effects>3D Effects>Cutout. Set the Shadow Colour to Black and deselect the 'Fill interior...' option

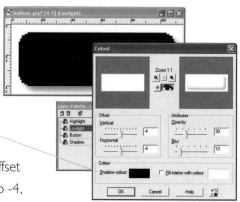

3 Try setting the Vertical offset to -4, Horizontal offset to -4, Opacity to 30 and Blur to 10. Click the Proof 👁 button to test the effect – you may need to modify the settings to suit your button. Click OK to apply the effect

4 Activate the Highlight layer. Make sure the selection is still active

You can also create 3D buttons using the Buttonize effect, but the results aren't as good. The other advantage of the Contour effect is that the selection boundary can be any shape, so you can use this method to create 3D text.

5 Apply the Cutout effect again, with the Shadow colour to white. Set the Vertical offset to 4, Horizontal offset to 4, Opacity to 40 and Blur to 10. Use the Proof button to check the highlight

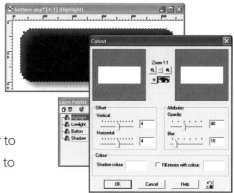

Adding text

The real beauty of layers is that you can store the text for all your buttons in a single file.

1 Add a new layer to the file. Call it Home and move it to the top of the heap. Make sure it's the active layer

2 Select the Text tool and click on the button. Enter the word 'Home' and format it. Set the Fill to white (or black, for a light-coloured button) and create it as Floating text

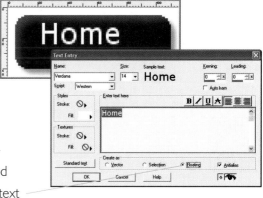

3 Move the text into place, then go to Selections>Defloat (or press Shift+Ctrl+F) to drop it back on to the Home layer. Deselect it

If the guide is hard to see, go to View>Change Grid and Guide Properties and change its colour.

4 If the rulers aren't displayed, go to View>Rulers to turn them on. Drag a guideline down from the top ruler and place it under the text

5 Click the Layer Visibility Toggle button for the Home layer to hide the text

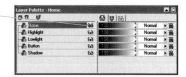

To create graphical buttons, paste simple images into the layers instead of inserting text. You can also use characters from the Webdings font, which contains common symbols.

6 Repeat Steps 1 to 3 to create another layer and add the text for the next button. Use the guideline to get it in the right place

7 Continue until you've entered the text for all your buttons, placing each piece of text in a separate layer

The great thing about layers is that it's easy to make changes. Don't like the drop shadow? Turn off that layer and export the buttons again. Wish you'd chosen a different colour? Activate the Button layer and use the Flood Fill tool to fill the basic shape with another colour.

8 Use the GIF Optimizer to save the buttons (see pages 76). Turn off all the text layers except the first one and export the file. Next, turn off all the text layers except the second one and export the file again, with a new name. Repeat until you've saved all the buttons

Inserting buttons

The easiest way to keep your buttons in order is to place them in a table with a single row and a column for each button.

1 Switch to Namo WebEditor and open your Web page

If you want the buttons spread out evenly across the page, set the Table Width to 100%. If you want them clumped in the centre, work out the total width in pixels (for example, five 115-pixel buttons gives a total width of 575 pixels) and use that number.

2 Go to Table>New Table. Set Rows to 1, Columns to the number you need (one per button) and Alignment to Center. Set Cell Padding, Cell Spacing and Border Thickness to 0 pixels

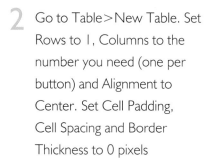

3 The table framework appears

Make sure all your files are in the right folders before you start inserting buttons and creating links.

4 Place the cursor in the first cell. Click the Insert Image button or go to Insert>Image

5 Find the image file for the first button. Check that Border thickness is set to 0

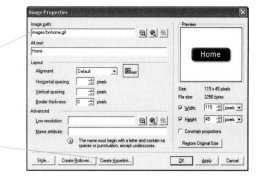

6 Click the Create Hyperlink button

If you need to enter an entire Web address, you must include the http:// *at the beginning.*

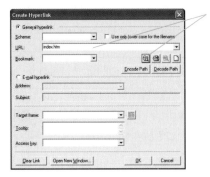

7 Click the Browse button and locate the file you want to link to (for a link to another Web site, enter the entire address)

8 Click OK twice to finish. Use the text-formatting tools to centre the button in the cell

9 Repeat Steps 4 to 8 to insert all the other buttons

10 Open the Web page in your Web browser(s) and make sure all the links work. Resize the browser window and check that all the buttons are still displayed

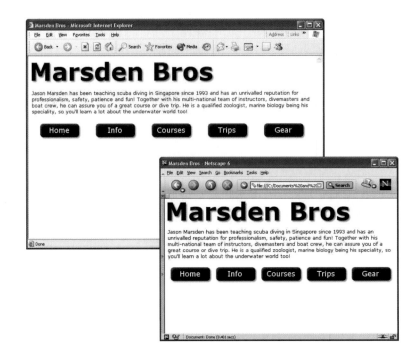

Horizontal rules

A 'rule' is a horizontal line that separates one section of a Web page from another.

You can create rules using HTML, by inserting an `<hr>` tag (or by selecting Insert>Horizontal Rule). However, the default rule is dull, the options are limited and the results vary between browsers.

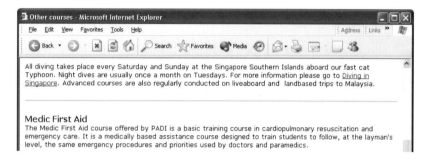

The alternative is to create a small graphic and stretch it out across the page, turning it into a rule. Many more styles and colours are possible using this approach. However, if you want your pages to look right on 640x480-pixel displays, you're limited to a maximum width of 590 pixels.

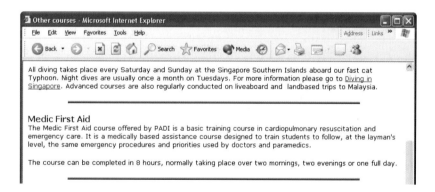

Creating a rule

Making your own rules is one of the easiest tasks in Web graphics.

You can create a smaller document if you wish. For example, the rule shown could be created from a 1x2-pixel file, stretched out to 590 pixels wide by 4 pixels high. However, very small images are difficult to work with, because they're hard to click on.

1 Open Paint Shop Pro and create a very small image – say, 10 pixels wide by 10 high

2 Zoom in on the image, then design your rule across the centre

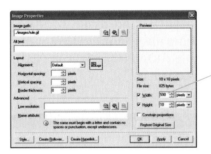

3 Export the image as a GIF

4 Switch to Namo WebEditor and open a Web page. Add an empty paragraph where the rule should appear

5 Insert the rule image into the new paragraph. Set the Width to 590 pixels to stretch the image. Set the Height to 10 pixels

6 Use the text-formatting tools to centre the rule

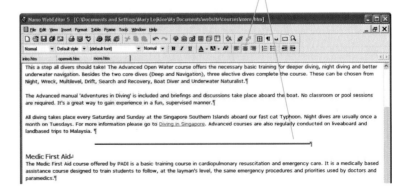

Bullets

HTML has a built-in 'bulleted list' paragraph format that inserts bullets. The bullets aren't exciting, but they're easy to add – just select the text and click the Bulleted List button.

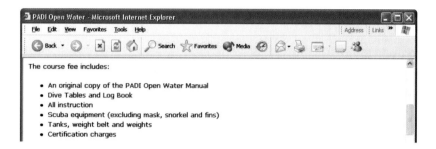

If you want more interesting bullets, you have to create your own. In general, it isn't worth the effort – not because they're difficult to create, but because they're a nuisance to insert. However, if your site won't be complete without colour-coordinated bullets, you can certainly have them. Create a simple graphic and insert it at the beginning of each paragraph.

There are a few things to remember when you're creating bullets:

- Add a few pixels of white space on the right-hand side of the file, to push the text away from the bullet

- If you don't want blank lines between the items, press Shift+Enter at the end of each line, rather than Enter.

- Once you've inserted the first bullet, select it and copy it. Paste it into the other paragraphs. All the HTML settings will be copied and pasted along with the image

Coloured backgrounds

Web pages don't have to have white backgrounds. You can change the colour or use a graphic to give a textured or patterned effect.

1 To change the background colour, run Namo WebEditor and go to File>Document Properties

2 Enter the hex value for a new Background colour (see page 30) or click the swatch to select a colour from the Web palette

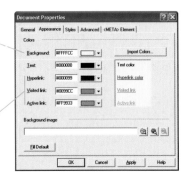

3 You might also want to change the Hyperlink, Visited link and Active link colours

4 You'll find that images with white backgrounds don't look right

Changing the background colour of your images is easy as long as you started with a transparent background (see page 70) and kept a copy of the Paint Shop Pro file, complete with all its layers.

5 Go back to Paint Shop Pro and edit the original images (the ones you saved in Paint Shop Pro format) so they have matching backgrounds. Add a new layer at the bottom of the heap and fill it with the background colour. Export the modified images as GIFs

Background images

If a coloured background isn't fancy enough, you can insert a background image. It will appear behind the text, repeating as many times as is necessary to fill the page.

Open Paint Shop Pro and create a simple, low-contrast image. Export it as a GIF

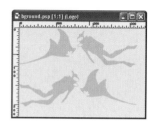

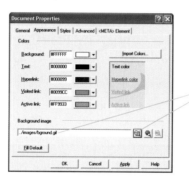

2 Switch to Namo WebEditor and go to File>Document Properties. Click the Browse button and locate your background image

3 The image is repeated (or 'tiled') all over the page, behind your text

Repeating images can be annoying and make your text difficult to read. Also, any headings, buttons or bullets you use must have transparent backgrounds – see page 141.

A more tasteful option is to use a background image to create panels of colour that support the structure of your page.

1   Go back to Paint Shop Pro and create a new image that's 1,600 pixels wide and 1 pixel high

2   Fill in the first 120 pixels with a browser-safe colour. Export the image as a GIF

3   Switch to Namo WebEditor and create a new Web page. Insert the new image as a background image. It repeats down the page, creating a coloured stripe

4   By using tables to control the placement of the text (see pages 107 and 147), you can turn the stripe into a coloured sidebar

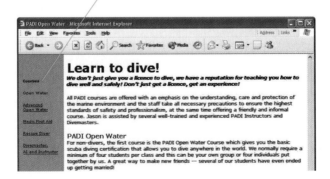

Seamless backgrounds

A third option is to give your Web page a textured or patterned background. To do this, you have to create a graphic that tiles (repeats) 'seamlessly', with no obvious joins. There are several ways to do this, depending on the type of background.

Cloudy backgrounds

A soft, marbled effect is quite easy to create and doesn't have too much effect on the readability of your text.

1   Create a new Paint Shop Pro document. Make it about 300x300 pixels and give it a white background

2   Select the Paint Brush ✎ tool. Set the Foreground Solid Colour to blue, the Size to 150, the Hardness to 0 and the Opacity to 25. Click about the document to make clouds

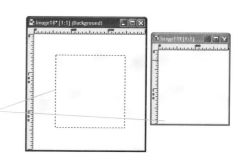

3   Select a square area in the centre of the image, then go to Selections> Convert to Seamless Pattern. Paint Shop Pro creates a new image

Background graphics with many colours and no lines or edges can be saved in the JPEG format. It gives better compression than the GIF format for this type of image.

4   Save the new image as a JPEG (see page 105) and use it as a background image

Stippled backgrounds

Slightly textured backgrounds can be created by adding noise.

1 Create a new 100x100-pixel image and fill it with a pale colour

2 Go to Effects>Noise>Add. Set the amount to 10% and the type to Uniform

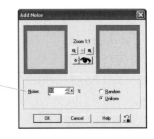

3 To mute the effect, go to Effects>Noise>Texture Preserving Smooth

4 Export the image as a JPEG and use it as a background

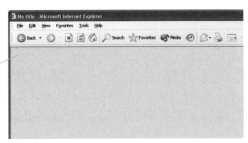

Patterned backgrounds

A patterned background isn't very practical, but it can be fun.

A 120x120-pixel image works well because it divides evenly into three, four, five, six or eight rows and columns.

1 Create a new 120x120-pixel image. Fill it with random brush strokes or use the Flood Fill tool to pour in a texture

2 Go to Effects>Reflection Effects> Pattern and experiment with different settings

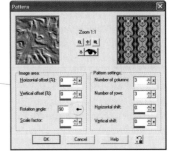

3 Export the pattern as a GIF and use it as a background

Photographs

This chapter explains how to use photographs on your Web site. As well as showing you how to acquire, edit, resize and save digital photographs, it covers specialised applications such as on-line galleries, cutouts, background images and wallpaper. It also explains how to set up a Webcam and add live, constantly updated images to your site.

Covers

Chapter Five

Introduction

There are lots of reasons for adding photographs to your Web site:

- They bring your Web site to life. No matter how scintillating your prose, a page of text looks dull. Photographs make your pages more appealing.

- They add credibility. Anyone can say they went sky diving or bungy-jumped off a bridge. Photographic evidence makes your stories easier to believe

- They supplement your descriptions. It's hard to recognise a person or place from a written description, but it's very easy when you've seen a photograph. If you want to help people find your business, add a photograph as well as a map, so they know when they've reached your building

- They show off your products. The problem with on-line shopping is that people can't handle the merchandise. With photographs, at least they can see what they're getting

- They show off your skills. If you're a keen photographer, adding pictures to your Web site is an easy way to share them with other enthusiasts

The main issue with photographs is size. Your digital images must be big enough (in pixels) to do justice to your subject, but small enough (in kilobytes) to download at a reasonable rate. Sometimes the best approach is to create two versions of each photo: a small preview image and a larger one that people can download if they want to see a sharper, more detailed image. First, though, you have to get the photographs on to your computer and convert them into a Web-friendly format.

Digital photographs

There are three ways to get photographs on to your computer:

- Capture them using a digital camera or Webcam

- Use a scanner to scan prints (or slides or negatives, if you opt for a film scanner)

- Ask your photo lab to copy the images on to a CD when it develops your film

Digital cameras

When you're in a hurry, a digital camera is the best solution. It enables you to put photographs on your Web site very quickly, at minimal cost (once you've paid for the camera). You can photograph a winter snowfall and have the pictures on your Web site before your snowman has melted. With a conventional camera, you might not finish the film until the summer. Also, if a picture doesn't turn out quite as well as you expected, you can take another one straight away.

Most digital cameras can capture images at several different sizes (or resolutions). Generally the smallest size is about right for photos that will be used on-line. However, you're better off selecting the largest size. Once you've adjusted the contrast and colours, and edited out any problems – such as unsightly rubbish bins and lampposts emerging from people's heads – you can resize the photograph for display on the Web (see page 104). The advantage of this approach is that small glitches introduced when you edit the image disappear when you resize it. If you capture the shot of a lifetime, the larger image also makes a nice print.

Scanners

There are two good reasons to own a flatbed scanner: they're relatively inexpensive and they enable you to convert existing photographs into computer files. They can also be used to digitise other material, such as sketches, brochures and maps.

Most scanners give you a choice of resolutions, ranging upwards from 75dpi. Although Web graphics are displayed at around 72dpi, it's best to scan at a resolution of 300dpi (or higher, if you want the screen image to be larger than the original). Once you've edited the image, you can reduce the resolution and resize it.

If you want the best possible scans – for example, because you're creating a Web site to show off your ability as a photographer – consider purchasing a film scanner. Although they are more expensive than flatbed scanners, film scanners enable you to work directly with your slides or negatives, which produces better results than scanning prints. On the downside, they aren't as versatile.

Photo-lab services

Although it's nice to have a scanner or a digital camera, and even nicer to have both, it isn't necessary. If you have any kind of 35mm or APS camera – even a disposable one – you can ask your photo lab to put the pictures on to a CD when it develops the film. Normally you get a set of conventional prints as well as the disc, so you can have the best of both worlds: prints to hand round and digital images to add to your Web site.

The best known film-to-disc service is Kodak's Picture CD service, which is available through many high-street photo labs (for more details, visit Kodak's Web site at `http://www.kodak.co.uk/`). Other companies have similar offerings, so if you don't use a Kodak lab, ask your current photo lab if it can put your pictures on to a disc. Normally you have to request this service when you have your film developed, although some labs also scan existing negatives. You can expect to pay a few pounds extra for the disc and you'll have to wait a few extra days to receive it.

Once again, the files on your disc will be too large (in pixel terms) to use on your Web site, so you'll need to resize them.

Copyright

Don't forget that other people's artwork is also covered by copyright. You can't scan anything you take a fancy to and add it to your Web site. For more information, visit the Web site of The Patent Office at `http://www.patent.gov.uk/copy/`

Images on the Web are protected by copyright. People can't just download your photographs and use them on their own Web sites or in printed material such as brochures or magazines – or rather, they can't *legally* download and reuse your pictures. From a practical point of view, photographs are vulnerable. You can't stop people from downloading them, you're unlikely to find out that your copyright has been violated, and suing people in other countries is difficult, to say the least.

There are several solutions to the copyright problem:

- Decide you don't care. Realistically, how desirable are your holiday snaps? It isn't worth losing sleep over photographs that have no commercial value

- Keep them small. Photographs are normally printed at a resolution of 300dpi, so a 300x200-pixel image ends up one inch (25mm) wide and less than three quarters of an inch (18mm) high. It's of limited use for printed material

To type a copyright symbol (©), hold down the Alt key and type 0169 on the numeric keyboard.

- Add a copyright symbol in one corner of the image, along with your name and the year. A thief can edit out your text, but it'll deter people who are reasonably honest or too lazy to do the editing. Try to put it on a textured area to make it difficult to remove

- Add a watermark across the middle of the image. Create a selection outline in the shape of your initials or logo, then use the Cutout technique covered on pages 84 and 85 to add highlights and shadows, giving an embossed effect. Watermarks are difficult to remove, but they also detract from your photograph

- Add a digital watermark that embeds your copyright information in the file. Digital watermarks don't alter the appearance of your photograph, but do enable you to prove ownership if it appears on another Web site. One option is Digimarc's ImageBridge system – see the Web site at `http://www.digimarc.com/` for details

Instant improvements

Although editing photographs is beyond the scope of this book, there are a couple of simple things you can do to improve them.

If your photo starts off as a JPEG, for example because it came from a digital camera, save it as a Paint Shop Pro (.psp) file before you start editing. You can then save it as you go, without compressing it. When you've finished, resize the image and save it as a JPEG (see pages 104 and 105). It's a good idea to keep the Paint Shop Pro version as a backup, in case you want to edit it again in the future.

1 Run Paint Shop Pro and open a digital photograph

2 Go to Colours> Adjust>Curves to bring up the Curves dialogue box

3 If the photo is too dark, click in the centre of the line to add a point, then drag it upwards and to the left to turn the line into a curve

4 If the photo lacks contrast, add two or three more points and drag them about to make an S-shaped curve. Click the Proof button to preview the result and adjust the curve if necessary

5 To correct the colours, go to Colours>Adjust>Colour Balance and adjust the sliders. The lighthouse looks slightly pink, so the highlights need a little less red and more green

You need to view the image in 1:1 mode to get an accurate preview of the Unsharp Mask effect.

6 If the photograph is already the right size, sharpen it (if you're going to resize it, do that first – see overleaf). Go to View>Normal Viewing so the image is displayed actual size, then go to Effects>Sharpen>Unsharp Mask

The name 'Unsharp Mask' comes from a technique used in traditional photography. In some programs the three settings are called Radius, Amount and Threshold. Unsharp Mask is by far the most effective of the sharpening tools, so don't bother with the others.

7 Try setting Radius to 1.00, Strength to 50 and Clipping to 5. Preview the results and adjust the settings. Increase the Radius and/or Strength for a more pronounced effect. Increase the Clipping if the image starts to look grainy

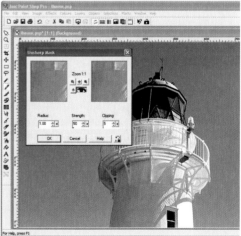

Resizing photographs

There are three things to remember when you're resizing photos:

*   When you make an image smaller, your image editor throws away the unwanted pixels and there's no easy way to get them back. Save the full-size version of the file, then resize it, then save the smaller version with a new name

One exception to this rule is that it's okay to resize the image a second time to make a thumbnail (see page 111), because you're changing the image size dramatically. What you don't want to do is make several small changes in pixel size.

*   For the best results, only resize the image once. If you want to shave off a few more pixels, try cropping the image. If that doesn't work, go back to the full-size version and start again

*   If you want the photograph to fit on a 640x480-pixel screen, limit the width to 590 pixels (see page 68). If you're placing it alongside text, you'll want it to be much smaller

Once the image has been resized, save it as a JPEG (see opposite).

1   To resize a photo, open it in Paint Shop Pro

Some image editors require you to specify a resolution when you resize a photograph. Use 72dpi, the approximate resolution of a computer screen.

2   Decide whether you really need everything you can see. If not, use the Crop ✄ tool to trim the image

3   Go to Image>Resize

Resizing makes a photograph look softer and slightly out of focus, so you'll need to sharpen it afterwards. Use the Unsharp Mask effect – see Steps 6 and 7 on the previous page.

4   Set Resize Type to Smart Size. Select the 'Resize all layers' and 'Maintain aspect ratio' checkboxes

5   Enter the new width. Paint Shop Pro calculates the new height (or vice versa)

6   Click OK to resize the photograph

Saving photographs

Photographs should be saved in the JPEG format (see page 40). The GIF format doesn't provide enough colours.

Complete all your editing and resizing before you convert your photograph into a JPEG. JPEG compression is lossy, so you lose some of the fine details when you save an image in this format – and there's no way to get them back.

1 To save a photo as a JPEG, go to File>Export>JPEG Optimizer

The greater the degree of compression, the smaller the file. In Paint Shop Pro, large numbers correspond to high degrees of compression and small files. In some other programs, large numbers correspond to low degrees of compression and large files. If you're in doubt, check the preview image.

2 Click the Quality tab and set the Compression value to a number between 1 (best quality, largest file) and 99 (worst quality, smallest file). Monitor the preview image and file size (on the right) to see the effect of your setting

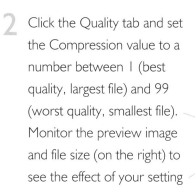

3 Click the Format tab. Select the Standard option for small photos. Use the Progressive option if you want to interlace large photos (see page 39)

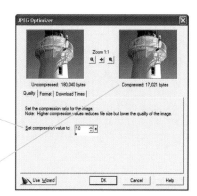

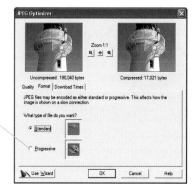

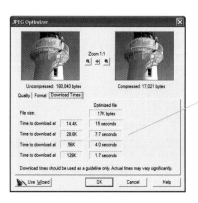

4 Click the Download Times tab and check the estimated times. If they seem too long, go back to Step 2 and increase the compression

Inserting photographs

Inserting photographs is no different from inserting other images.

1 Check that both the photograph and the Web page have been saved into the correct folder(s)

2 Place the cursor in the correct position, then click the Insert Image button or go to Insert>Image

3 Locate the image file and fill in the Alt text

4 Some photographs look better with a narrow line around the edge. Set Border to 1 pixel to add one

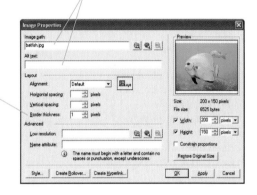

You can't control the colour of the border. Also, the border is added outside the image, making it 2 pixels wider, which may cause problems in very precise layouts. A more reliable way to add a border is to use your image editor to add a line of black pixels around the edge of the image file.

5 The image is inserted, complete with border

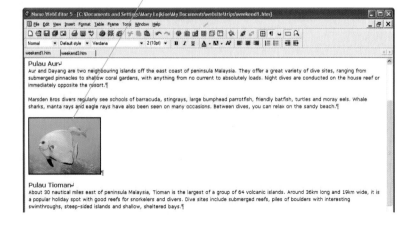

Text flow

HTML gives you only limited control over the relative placement of text and photographs. When you're designing a page that combines the two, you have three options:

- Place the photos between paragraphs of text (see opposite)

See page 57 for more on aligning images.

- Place each photo alongside a paragraph of text, on either the left or the right. The problem with this option is that the text may not flow smoothly down the page

Chapter 7 covers more sophisticated techniques for controlling the layout of your page.

- Use a table to separate the photos from the text. This is the most versatile option. The text runs on continuously, so it's easy to read. It's also easy to add captions

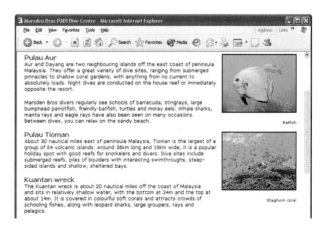

To create separate areas for text and photographs, insert a simple table with one row and two columns.

1 Open a Web page and create a new table. Set Width to 100%

2 You don't want the text right up against the photos, so set Cell padding and Cell spacing to 5 pixels. Set the Border Thickness to 0 pixels

If you're adding captions, they should be narrower than the photos. Press Shift+Enter to insert line breaks if necessary.

3 Place the text in one column and the photographs and captions in the other

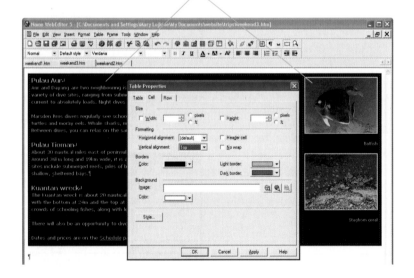

You can't set the cell alignment when you create the table, so you have to go back and change it afterwards. If you don't bother, strange things will happen when one column contains more material than the other.

4 Select the entire table, then right-click on it and select Cell Properties from the pop-up menu. Change the Vertical alignment to Top so everything lines up at the top of the page

Thumbnails and galleries

When you have a lot of photographs to display, the best option is to create an index page with small 'thumbnail' versions. People can get an overview of your collection, then click on individual thumbnails to load larger versions of the images that interest them. You can include text on the page with the thumbnails or with the individual images.

If you're telling a story, it's better to put all the text on one page. If the photos are loosely related and can be viewed in any order, put the text with the images.

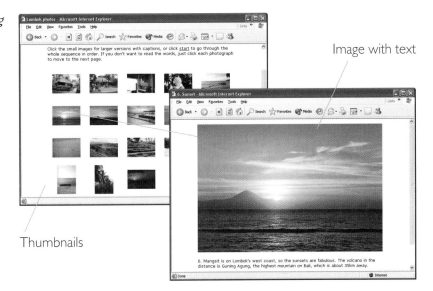

Image with text

Thumbnails

Isolated image

Thumbnails with text

There are several things to think about when you're making thumbnails:

- Decide on a naming scheme. For example, you might use the name of the original file, but with a 't' on the end

- Keep them small! You can compromise on both the pixel size and the image quality to reduce the file size. The thumbnail just has to give people a rough idea of what they'll see when they click through to the larger version

- Even small files take time to download, so don't put too many thumbnails on one page. If you have a lot of photos, sort them into categories and make several index pages

- Normally a thumbnail is just a miniature version of the full-size photo. However, sometimes it makes sense to crop the photograph before you shrink it. For example, if you turn a full-length portrait into a tiny thumbnail, the subject is hard to recognise. It's better to crop in on their face

- Cropping is also useful if you have a lot of landscape ('wide') images and just one or two in portrait ('tall') format. You can crop the portrait photos to produce landscape thumbnails

- If you have an even mixture of landscape and portrait photographs, consider adding white borders to the thumbnails so all the image files are square. The borders compress well, so they don't contribute much to the file size, and they make it easier to lay out the index page

1 To create a thumbnail, open a digital photo. Resize it so the longest side is between 50 and 120 pixels

2 To add white borders, set the Background Solid Colour to white. Go to Image>Canvas Size and increase the width and height

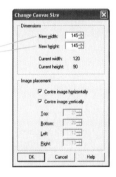

3 Export the image as a JPEG. Compress it well and don't forget to give it a new name!

4 Make thumbnails for all your photos, then switch to Namo WebEditor. Insert a table with enough cells for all your thumbnails

If your thumbnails don't have white borders, set Cell spacing to about 20 pixels to separate the images from each other. You'll need to allow for the spacing when you calculate the width.

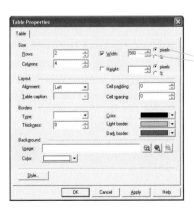

5 Specify the table's width in pixels, by multiplying the number of columns by the width of each thumbnail

6 Set Cell padding to 0, Cell spacing to 0 and Border Thickness to 0 pixels

7 Insert your images, one per table cell

8 Right-click on a
thumbnail and
select Create
Hyperlink. You
can link directly to
the larger version
of the photograph
or to a Web page
containing the larger
version. To link to
the image file, click
the Browse button.
Set Files of Type to All Files, then select the file

The advantage of linking directly to the larger version of the
photograph is that you don't have to make lots of Web pages.
However, you end up with a primitive navigation system. People
have to click on a thumbnail, then use their browser's Back button
to return to the index, and then click on another thumbnail. This
approach is okay when you have photographs illustrating a report
or on-line catalogue, because people won't want to see the full-size
version of every image. If you're expecting people to look at all
your photos, it's better to create a separate Web page for each image
and link the thumbnails to the pages. You can then include links
that enable people to go back to the index or on to the next picture
in the sequence. You can also include explanatory text. Although
it's more work, it makes your gallery much easier to browse.

Cutouts

A cutout is a photo that has had its background removed, making it an irregular shape. It looks as if the person or object has been 'cut out' using scissors and pasted on to a blank page.

The best way to make a cutout is to photograph the subject against a plain white background. You don't need any fancy equipment – a large sheet of white paper will do. If possible, go outside or work next to window, so you can use natural light, and use a tripod to keep the camera steady. Avoid taking pictures on a very bright day or using a flash, because you'll end up with harsh shadows. Even, diffuse lighting produces soft shadows that are more attractive and easier to work with. Ideally they should fall downwards and to the right, so they match the drop shadows on your headings.

Cutting someone (or something) out of a scene is much harder, because there's no easy way to select the background. It takes so much longer to achieve a good result that it's usually quicker to go out and take a new photograph.

Once you've taken a suitable photograph and transferred it on to your computer, open it in Paint Shop Pro

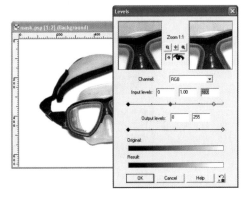

2 Go to Colours > Adjust > Levels. Drag the white diamond to the left until the background is more-or-less white

You can also use the Magic Wand to select any shadows cast by the object, so they are deleted along with the background. However, cutouts often look more natural with the shadows left in.

If the photo is about the right size, use a 1-pixel feather. If you're going to reduce the size, increase the feathering.

3 Use the Magic Wand tool to select the background. You may need to use the Freehand tool to tidy up the edges of the selection or select groups of darker pixels that the Wand has missed

4 Go to Selections>Invert or press Ctrl+Shift+I to invert the selection

5 Go to Selections>Modify>Feather and feather the selection by 1 to 3 pixels

6 Invert the selection again. Make sure the Background Solid Colour is set to white, then delete the selected area

7 Crop, resize and sharpen the image, as required

8 Export the image as a JPG and use it on your Web pages

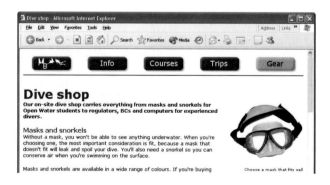

Background images

You can also use a photograph as the background image for your Web page. However, it needs to be large, so a single repeat fills the window, and it needs to be very pale, so your text is still legible.

People with small screens will only see the top left-hand corner of the background image, so ideally you want an abstract photograph that provides all-over interest, such as a shot of autumn leaves spread across the grass.

1 Crop and/or resize your photograph so it's 1,024 pixels high by 768 wide. At this size it will fill the browser window on all but the very largest of computer screens

2 Display the Layer Palette. You need to move the photo off the background layer, so go to Selections> Select All (or press Ctrl+A), then press Ctrl+X to cut the photograph. Go to Edit>Paste>As New Layer (or press Ctrl+L) to paste it back into a new layer

3 Drag the new layer's Opacity slider to the left to make the photo lighter

4 Export the photo as a JPEG. You'll need to choose a high compression level to keep the file size down

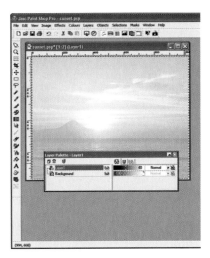

5 Use the photograph as a background image (see page 93 and overleaf)

Wallpaper

If you have photographs you're particularly proud of, consider giving them away as Windows wallpaper. All you need to do is create files for the most popular screen resolutions – 800x600 and 1,074x768 pixels – and make them available via your Web site.

1 Convert your best pictures into wallpaper-sized files, then make a thumbnail for each one

2 Create a Web page that catalogues the available images. Use text links that go straight to the appropriate file

3 It's a good idea to include some instructions. Tell people to follow the link for the file they want to install. When the image appears in their browser window, they should right-click on it. Internet Explorer users simply have to select Set as Background. Netscape users should select Save Image and save the image into their My Pictures folder. They can then right-click on their desktop, select Properties and click the Desktop tab to change their wallpaper

Live photographs

For links to hundreds of sites with live images, visit the EarthCam Web site at `http://www.earthcam.com/`

You've probably come across Web sites that display live images of city skylines, famous landmarks, sports arenas and office interiors. The picture is updated every few seconds, minutes or hours so you can follow the action or admire the view.

If you have a Webcam attached to your computer, it's relatively easy to configure your system to take photographs at regular intervals and upload them to your Web site. You need five things to get started:

- **A Webcam** (see page 17). It doesn't need to be anything fancy because you'll only be capturing low-resolution stills

- **Software** to control the camera and upload the images. You may get a suitable program with your camera, or you can purchase third-party applications such as ISpy (available from Surveyor Corporation at `http://www.ispy.nl/`)

- **An Internet connection.** Ideally you want a permanent, 'always on' connection, but you can use a dial-up connection – most programs can be configured to dial your service provider, upload the latest image and then drop the line

- **FTP access** to your Web space. You'll need to enter the address of your Web server and your password and username when you configure the software

- **An interesting view.** The point of setting up a camera is to create a page that changes regularly, so people are encouraged to come back to your Web site. Interior shots aren't ideal, because people in offices do the same thing every day. With an exterior shot, the view changes with the time of day, the weather, the time of year and so on. You could also set up a short-term camera to cover a specific event, such as a festival, the construction of a new building or a birth at your local zoo

Software configuration

Once your Webcam and software are installed, you can start setting things up. The screen grabs show Surveyor Corporation's ISpy (see previous page for details), but other programs have similar options.

1 Run ISpy and go to File>Settings. Choose your connection type. If you use a modem and have more than one Internet account, select the one you want ISpy to use

2 Click the FTP tab and enter the address of your Web space, your password and your user name

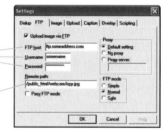

As always, consider the structure of your site and the rules for naming folders and files – see page 48.

3 Tell ISpy where to put the image and what to call it

4 Click the Image tab and set the Image Quality (the higher the quality, the lower the compression and the larger the file)

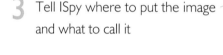

Many Web-space providers limit the amount of data that you can transfer each day. If you're uploading an image every minute, and you have several visitors downloading it every minute, you may exceed your allowance.

5 Click the Upload tab and set up a schedule. The frequency depends on your scene. For a static view, once an hour might be enough. In a location with lots of activity, you might update once a minute

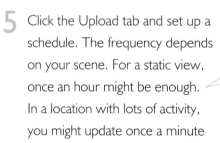

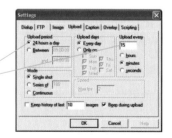

6 Click OK to return to the main ISpy window

Pick a scene that is more interesting than this one!

7 Check that the camera is focused and pointing in the right direction

8 To change the size of the image, go to Video>Format. Select a new resolution

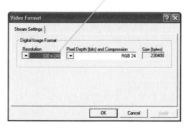

9 ISpy starts capturing and uploading images

Designing the Web page

Simply uploading the images to your Web space isn't much use. You also need to design a Web page so people can view them.

1 Run Namo WebEditor, create a new Web page, and save it

Alternatively, use your image editor to create a file that's the right pixel size and has the right name. It can just be a coloured rectangle, because it's only a dummy file to help you design the Web page.

2 You'll need a sample image to put on the page. ISpy saves the latest image on to your hard disk, in the C:\Program Files\ISpy folder. Use Windows Explorer to copy this file into the folder with your pages

3 Add the image to your Web page, along with a caption and any other relevant material

If you've been using a visual HTML editor, editing the code by hand may seem like a big step. However, the best way to learn is to plunge in and have a go. Make a back-up copy of the file first, then switch to HTML mode and start typing.

The <head> and </head> tags create an area for details that do not appear on the Web page, such as the page title. The <meta> tag normally holds information about the contents of the page, but can also be used to refresh it.

4 To make the page reload itself at regular intervals, click the HTML tab to edit the code directly. Somewhere between the `<head>` and `</head>` tags, add a line that says:

```
<meta http-equiv="refresh" content="900">
```

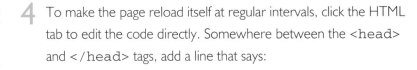

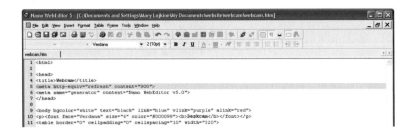

The `content` attribute specifies the time between refreshes, in seconds, so `content="900"` refreshes the page every 15 minutes. Change this number to match the upload interval you chose in Step 5 on page 118

The image keeps changing because ISpy overwrites the old image with a new one at regular intervals. If your image isn't being updated, it's probably because the files aren't being uploaded to the correct place. To keep things simple, put the HTML document and the image file in the same folder.

5 Upload the page to your Web server. Check that ISpy is running, then visit the page and watch your live images appear

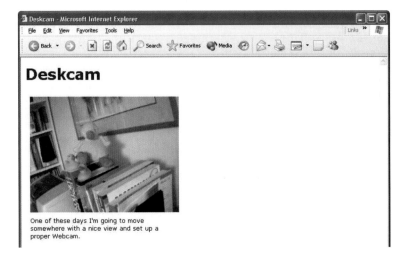

One of these days I'm going to move somewhere with a nice view and set up a proper Webcam.

Interactive graphics

This chapter covers three tricks that make your Web site more interactive: image maps, rollovers and favicons. You'll also learn more about editing the HTML directly and get a quick introduction to JavaScript.

Covers

Chapter Six

Introduction

So far the only interactive graphics you've encountered are buttons and thumbnails – images that are hyperlinked so a click takes you to another page or image. This chapter deals with two more sophisticated types of interactive graphic:

- **An image map** is a graphic with multiple clickable areas. Each area is linked to a different target – either a different Web page or a different section of the same page. For example, clicking on one of the destinations marked on this map takes you to a description of it

- **A rollover** is a graphic that changes when the mouse passes over it and/or when it is clicked. For example, these buttons change colour when the mouse pointer passes over them. Rollovers provide feedback – the change of colour implies that the mouse pointer is in the right place and something will happen when you click

This chapter also explains how to make a favicon – an icon that is added to Internet Explorer's Favorites menu when someone makes a shortcut for your site.

Image maps

Image maps present choices visually. They are more attractive than lists of links and can also be more intuitive. People simply look at the map, spot the item they're interested in and click on it.

The most obvious application for an image map is an actual map of an area or building, with links to information about the places shown. However, you don't have to be that literal. If you're creating a Web site about a group of people, you could take a photograph of everyone and link each person's face to their section of the site.

Image maps can also be visual metaphors. For example, you might open a personal Web site with a photograph of the items on your desk: diary, box of index cards, camera, computer and so on. You could link the diary to your on-line diary, the box of cards to your contact details, the camera to a gallery of photographs, the computer to a list of your favourite Web sites, and so on.

There are two important considerations when you're creating image maps:

- It must be obvious that the graphic is clickable. If it isn't, people may pass by without following the links. Sometimes you need to add a line of text that tells visitors what to do

- It should be clear which items are clickable and what they lead to. Be careful with visual metaphors. If you make them too complicated or obscure, people end up clicking around at random, hoping to find something interesting

Adding hotspots

To turn a graphic into an image map, you have to define clickable areas or 'hotspots'. The procedure depends on your program, but generally you select the area you want to activate, then assign a Web address. Once you've defined all the hotspots, the program produces a fragment of HTML that you can add to your Web page.

1 Open Paint Shop Pro, then open the image you want to use

2 Go to File>Export> Image Mapper

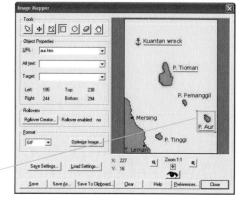

Allow some leeway for sloppy clicking, but try to leave a gap between clickable areas so people don't end up on the wrong page.

3 To mark out a regular area, select the Rectangle ☐ or Circle ○ tool. Draw round the area you want to select

4 If necessary, use the Arrow ▧ and/or Mover ✛ tools to adjust the boundary

5 Enter the address of the page you want to link to. You can enter a full or partial address, depending on the location of the page

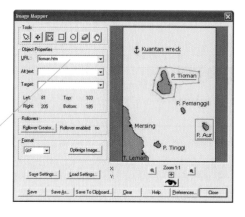

If the image doesn't already have labels, you can add Alt text for the clickable areas.

6 To mark an irregular area, use the Polygon ▨ tool to click round the area you want to select. Each click becomes a corner

7 Add the address

8 Once you've defined all the hotspots, set the image format to GIF or JPEG. Click the Optimize Image button

9 Adjust the number of colours or the compression value, as appropriate (see pages 76 and 105). Click OK to go back to the Image Mapper

Saving the settings is akin to keeping copies of your images in Paint Shop Pro format. You don't need the settings file for your Web site, but it's useful to have it if you need to make changes to the map.

10 Click the Save Settings button to save the map areas and addresses, in case you need to reload them and make changes

11 Click the Save button to create a HTML document containing the image map. You'll also be prompted to save the image itself. Keep things simple by putting them both in the same folder

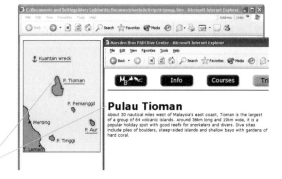

You can also create image maps in Namo WebEditor. Insert an image, then go to View> Toolbars>Image. The hotspot tools are similar to Paint Shop Pro's.

12 Open the HTML file in your Web browser and check that the hotspots behave as you intended

Using image maps

One way to use your image map is to open the HTML document in your Web editor and add text, other graphics and so on to complete the page. However, that's inconvenient if you've already designed a page and just want to drop the map into place. The alternative is to copy the HTML into your existing document.

To display the documents side by side, go to Window>Tile Vertically.

1 Open both documents in Namo WebEditor

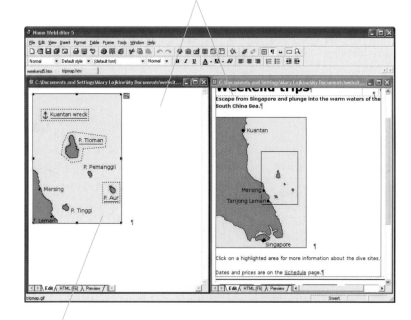

2 Click on the image map to select it, then copy it

For the cut-and-paste approach to work, you must keep your files and folders in order. When you save the map document (Step 11, previous page), put it into the same folder as the document you want to copy the map into.

3 Paste it into the other document. Namo WebEditor copies the hotspot details as well as the image

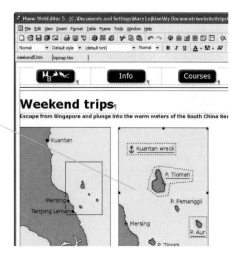

Other Web editors may not be as smart, in which case you'll have to transfer the map details by hand.

1 Open both documents. Insert the map image in the existing Web page

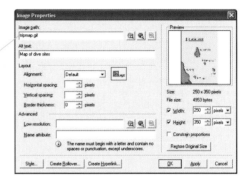

2 Click on the image in the map document, then switch to HTML view. Do the same thing for the image in the existing Web page. The HTML that describes the image should be highlighted

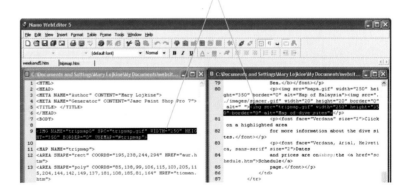

The name *attribute is used when you need to be able to refer to a specific image from another part of the document. The* usemap *attribute tells the browser where to find the hotspot information.*

3 Compare the two `<img>` tags. The tag for the map has two extra attributes:

```
NAME="tripmap0"

USEMAP="#tripmap"
```

Copy those attributes to the `<img>` tag in the other document

4 At the bottom of the map document you'll find the code that specifies the hotspots, enclosed in `<map>` and `</map>` tags:

```
<MAP NAME="tripmap">
<AREA SHAPE="rect" COORDS="195,238,244,
294" HREF="aur.htm">
<AREA SHAPE="poly" COORDS="85,138,99,
106,115,103,205,115,204,144,142,149,
137,181,108,185,81,164" HREF=
"tioman.htm">
<AREA SHAPE="rect" COORDS="25,43,159,
74" HREF="kuantan.htm">
</MAP>
```

Copy the entire block to the other document. Place it at the end, immediately before the `</body>` tag

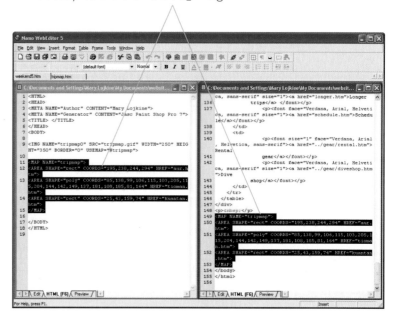

5 Save the modified document, then open it in your Web browser and check that the image map functions correctly

Image rollovers

Rollover effects are created using JavaScript, a scripting language that can be used to add interactive elements to your Web pages. JavaScript enables you to add scrolling messages, change the background colour, generate pop-up windows, perform simple calculations and so on. The extra instructions or 'scripts' are added to the HTML document.

A 'rollover' is created using a simple script that's activated when the mouse 'rolls over' the target object. The most common example is a script that replaces one image file with another, so the graphic appears to change when the mouse touches it. If you've come across buttons that change colour when your mouse pointer approaches them, you've seen rollovers in action. Rollovers are also known as 'mouseovers', for obvious reasons.

Many image editors and HTML editors can create image rollovers for you. You select the images, they generate the script and your page comes alive. Alternatively, you can create the script yourself.

To create a rollover, you need two images that are identical in size, but different in appearance. If you create buttons using layers (see page 83), it's easy to change the colour of the background layer to produce a second, contrasting version. Alternatively, add a coloured glow to the second image so the button appears to 'light up' when the mouse approaches.

To create a glow, follow the instructions on page 83 to create a layered button. Instead of adding a drop shadow, duplicate the 'Button' layer. Select the bottom copy and apply the Gaussian Blur effect with a Radius of 2 to 4 pixels.

Easy rollovers

The easy way to create a rollover is to use a program that does most of the work for you, such as Namo WebEditor.

1 Open the Web page that contains the first image

2 Right-click on the image and select Image Properties. Click the Create Rollover button at the bottom of the dialogue box

The name must be unique. If you want to use the same button elsewhere on this page, you'll have to give it a different name.

3 Give the image a name

4 Click the Browse button and locate the second image file

5 Run your mouse over the Preview image to test the rollover

6 Click Finish and OK, then save the Web page and check the rollover effect in your Web browser

Writing your own code

To learn more about JavaScript, look out for another book in this series 'JavaScript in easy steps', or visit JavaScript Developer Central at `http://developer.netscape.com/tech/javascript/index.html`

Writing your own rollover instructions takes a little longer. However, it isn't difficult and it's a good introduction to scripting. Writing your own code enables you to create more sophisticated rollovers. For example, instead of changing the graphic that the mouse passes over, you can change one of the other graphics on the page (see page 134).

1 Start by assembling the components of your rollover. Note down the filename and location of each of the graphics

2 Insert the first image, and turn it into a link, in the usual way

3 Click on the image to select it, then switch to HTML view and find the corresponding `<img>` tag. You need to give the image a name so you can refer to it in the rollover script. Add a `name` attribute at the beginning of the `<img>` tag:

```
name="courses1"
```

4 Go up to the top of the document. Add the following code,
immediately above the </head> tag:

```
<script language="JavaScript">
<!--

// -->
</script>
```

The <script> and </script> tags create a container for
your code, and language=JavaScript tells your browser
that you are using JavaScript (there are several other scripting
languages). The <!-- and // --> hide the script from older
browsers that won't understand it

*Change the
variable names,
filenames and
file locations to
suit your own
images. Use meaningful
names for the variables –
in this example, the variable
name is the name given to
the image, plus 'over' or
'out' to indicate when the
image is displayed.*

5 Within the <script> tags, add the following code:

```
var courses1over=new Image();
courses1over.src="../images/courseso.
gif";
var courses1out=new Image();
courses1out="../images/coursesb.gif";
```

This code creates two image variables and loads them with the
two images. Courses1over contains the image that should be
displayed when the mouse is over the button – the orange button.
Courses1out contains the image that should be displayed when

the mouse moves away again – the regular blue button. When your Web browser reads this piece of code, it downloads both the images so they are ready for use in the rollover

The rollover code goes inside the `<a href>` tag, not the `<img>` tag.

6 Go back down the document and find the `<a href>` tag that specifies the link (it should be immediately before the `<img>` tag. Add the following code, after the details of the linked page:

```
onMouseOver="document.courses1.src=
courses1over.src;"
onMouseOut="document.courses1.src=
courses1out;"
```

If you look at the code for a rollover created by Namo WebEditor (see page 130), you'll find it looks different. Namo WebEditor uses a more complicated script that is more efficient when there are several rollovers on a page.

This code tells the browser that when the mouse is over the area that activates the link (that is, over the button), it should change the image called `courses1` to the image stored in the variable `courses1over`. When the mouse moves off the image, it should display the image stored in `courses1out`

7 Save the document and test your rollover in your Web browser

Changing another image

Suppose your toolbar has a row of buttons, plus an icon at the end which changes when you change sections.

Rather than changing the Trips button when someone moves their mouse over it, you want to replace the mask icon with another icon depicting a fin. To do this, you add rollover code to the Trips button, but you tell the browser to change the icon image.

Collect up your images, as before:

../images/maskicon.gif

../images/finicon.gif

../images/tripb.gif

The graphic that activates the rollover (that is, the graphic the mouse will pass over to trigger the effect) has to be linked to something, because the code has to go in an `<a href>` *tag. If the graphic you want to use isn't linked, you can add a dummy link that doesn't go anywhere. To do this, select the graphic and add a link in the usual way, entering a hash sign (#) for the address.*

2 Insert the button and turn it into a link.

3 Insert the icon and add a `name` attribute to its `<img>` tag:

```
name="icon1"
```

4 Follow Steps 4 and 5 on page 132. The code that declares the variables should be:

```
var icon1over=new Image();
icon1over.src="../images/finicon.gif";
var icon1out=new Image();
icon1out="../images/maskicon.gif";
```

This code is added to the `<a href>` tag belonging to the image that activates the rollover – in this case, the Trips button. You don't have to do anything to the tags for the image you want to change, other than add a name (Step 3).

5 Go back down the document and find the `<a href>` tag that specifies the link for the button. Add the following code:

```
onMouseOver="document.icon1.src=
icon1over.src;"
onMouseOut="document.icon1.src=
icon1out;"
```

6 Test the rollover. When the mouse is over the button, the browser should change the image called `icon1` (the icon image)

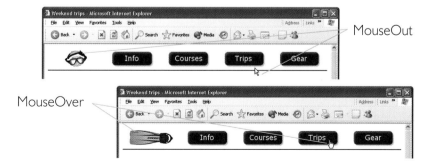

Favicon

A 'favicon' or 'Favorites icon' is a customised icon that is added to Internet Explorer's Favorites menu when someone makes a shortcut for your Web site. It is displayed in place of the usual 'e' icon.

The favicon also appears on the desktop if someone creates a shortcut there, and it's displayed at the beginning of the Address bar when the person revisits your site.

Creating a favicon

To create a favicon, you'll need a program that can save graphics in the Windows icon format (.ico). The simplest option is to use a dedicated icon editor, such as Microangelo from Impact Software (http://www.impactsoft.com/).

There are several standard sizes for icons, ranging from 16x16 pixels up to 48x48 pixels, and they can have 16, 256 or 16.7 million colours. For a favicon, it's best to use the most basic settings: 16x16 pixels and 16 colours.

1   Run Microangelo and create a new icon

2   Go to Tools>New Image Format. Set the Color Depth to 16 Color and the Size to 16x16

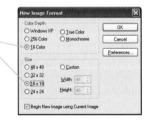

3   Click the Preferences button, then click the Transparency tab

4   Set the Background Color to pale grey, the default colour for Windows menus. Click OK twice to go back to the main window

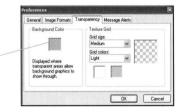

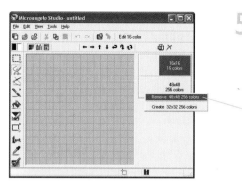

5 You should have a panel on the right that says '16x16, 16 colors'. Right-click on any other panels and remove any other formats, so you're just creating a basic icon

6 Use the painting tools to design your icon

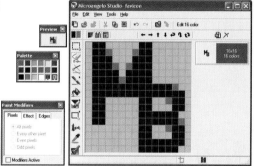

7 Go to File>Save As and save your icon. Call it `favicon.ico` and save it as an Icon Resource

Using your favicon

If you have your own domain name and your Web address is `http://www.yourname.com/` (or something similar), using your favicon is easy. Simply place the `favicon.ico` file in your top folder – the one that contains your `index.htm` file (see page 50). Internet Explorer will track it down whenever someone adds one of your pages to their Favorites menu. The same icon is used for all the pages from your site.

If you don't have your own domain name and your Web address is something like `http://www.someisp.com/yourname/`, using your favicon is slightly more complicated. Instead of placing the icon in the main folder and relying on Internet Explorer locating it, you have to add some code to your Web pages that tells the browser where to look.

1 Decide where you're going to keep the `favicon.ico` file – in your images folder, perhaps

2 Run Namo WebEditor and open a Web page. Switch to HTML view so you can edit the code directly

3 Somewhere between the `<head>` and `</head>` tags, add the following line of code:

This is one occasion when it makes sense to give the complete address of the image file. That way you can copy the statement to all your other pages, without worrying about the relative location of the icon file.

```
<link rel="shortcut icon" href=
"http://www.someisp.com/yourname/
images/favicon.ico">
```

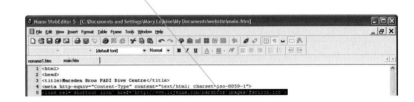

4 Copy this statement to all your other pages

This method is also useful if your Web site has several distinct sections. You can create multiple icons with different names, then edit the statement so it refers to the particular icon you want to use for each page.

Page layout

This chapter covers two tricks that can be used to improve the appearance of your pages: transparency and image slicing. It also deals with general layout issues, including the best way to use tables.

Covers

Chapter Seven

Introduction

Designing Web pages can be frustrating. You spend ages arranging text and pictures in your HTML editor, getting everything lined up perfectly – and then when you load the page into your Web browser, nothing is quite where you wanted it to be.

Designing for the Web is different from designing for print. With most desktop-publishing programs, what you see on the screen is what you get on the printed page. The layout of the document certainly doesn't change after you have printed it. The locations of all the items on the page are specified very precisely, so if you print 100 copies, they all look exactly the same.

When you're designing Web pages, you don't have as much control over the final layout. When someone views one of your Web pages, their browser automatically adapts it to suit their screen. Different Web browsers also interpret your instructions slightly differently.

The bottom line is that you can't make your Web pages look exactly the same on every computer. Attempting to control the layout very precisely is counterproductive, because it makes the pages less flexible. The more effort you expend on making your pages 'pixel perfect' on your own screen, the more likely it is they'll look terrible on other people's. It's better to keep things simple and accept that people with different systems will get slightly different views of your material. It's the content that counts, after all.

That said, there are ways to improve the layout of your pages without making them inflexible. This chapter deals with two of them:

- **Transparency** enables you to create irregular graphics that work on any background. Transparent images can also be used to separate other items and to control the column widths and row heights in a table

- **Image slicing** enables you to combine graphics with editable text to create magazine-style layouts. It can also be used to create sophisticated interactive images

Transparency

When you save a graphic in the GIF format, you can make parts of it transparent. If you place it on a coloured background, the background 'shows through' the transparent areas (see page 33). The graphic appears to have an irregular shape.

Transparency is useful when you want to use a logo or heading on several different backgrounds, or on a patterned or textured background. The main limitation is that the graphic must have 'clean' edges. Transparency doesn't combine well with anti-aliasing (see page 34) or soft drop shadows (see page 74). Light-coloured pixels at the edge of the object or its shadow remain opaque, creating a 'halo' effect on dark backgrounds.

Marsden — No anti-aliasing

Marsden — Anti-aliasing and shadow

You can use dithering to convert a soft shadow into a hardish one that'll display correctly (see page 143). Don't use anti-aliasing on headings and logos if you're planning to give them transparent backgrounds, because there's no easy way to get rid of it.

If all your pages have white backgrounds, you don't need to bother with transparency – just give your graphics white backgrounds, so they blend into the page. If your pages have coloured backgrounds, but they're all the same colour – pale yellow, say – you can either give your graphics matching backgrounds or use transparency. Using transparency makes it easy to replace the yellow with another colour.

There are two ways to make part of a graphic transparent:

- Design it on a transparent background and preserve the transparency when you save it as a GIF

- Fill the background with a colour that isn't used anywhere else in the document, then replace that colour with transparency when you save the image

Creating transparent graphics

The easiest way to create a graphic with a transparent background is to start from scratch.

While you're designing, be careful that you don't fill in the background with a solid colour.

1 Run Paint Shop Pro and create a new image. Set the background colour to Transparent

2 Design your heading, logo or other graphic

3 Go to File>Export> GIF Optimizer. In the Transparency section, select 'Existing image or layer transparency'

4 Optimise the colours and save the image (see page 76)

5 Test the graphic on a Web page with a coloured background

Dealing with shadows

When you add a soft shadow to a heading or logo, you end up with a fringe of semi-transparent pixels around the edge. However, the GIF format doesn't support degrees of transparency – pixels are either see-through or opaque. When you save the image, you have to decide what to do with the semi-transparent pixels.

It only makes sense to add a shadow if you'll be using the image on light-coloured backgrounds. If your pages have dark backgrounds, don't bother.

1 Design your graphic on a transparent background and give it a soft drop shadow (see page 74)

2 Go to File>Export>GIF Optimizer. In the Transparency section, select 'Existing image or layer transparency'

3 Click the Partial Transparency tab. To turn the soft shadow into a hard shadow, select the 'Use full transparency for pixels below…' option

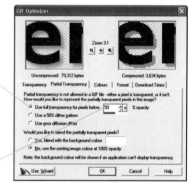

4 Adjust the cutoff percentage to control the size of the shadow

5 Alternatively, choose one of the dithering options. These options give the shadow a fuzzy, splatter-painted edge

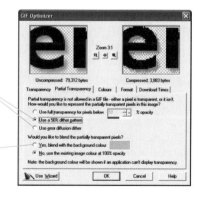

If your text is anti-aliased, select the 'No, use the existing colour…' option.

6 For a softer effect, select the 'Yes, blend with…' option. Set the background to a lighter shade of grey (*don't* use white)

7 Optimise the colours and save the graphic

...cont'd

Retrospective transparency

If you didn't plan ahead and design your graphic on a transparent background, don't panic. You can fill in the background with a solid colour, then make that colour transparent when you convert the image into a GIF.

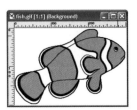

Open the graphic in Paint Shop Pro

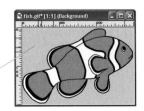

Sometimes you can use the existing background colour as the transparent colour. However, all instances of that colour will be removed. If white was used as the transparent colour for the fish graphic, the white areas on the body of the fish would also become see-through.

2 Select a colour that doesn't appear anywhere in the image. Fill all the areas that should be transparent

3 Go to File>Export>GIF Optimizer. In the Transparency section, select 'Areas that match this colour'. Click the coloured swatch and select the colour you used to fill the background

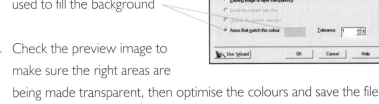

4 Check the preview image to make sure the right areas are being made transparent, then optimise the colours and save the file

144 | Web graphics in easy steps

Transparent spacers

A small, square, completely transparent image is useful as a spacer. You can use the Width and Height properties (see pages 55 and 90) to adjust its size and create precisely the gap you require.

Some people use 1x1-pixel images and scale them as required. However, a 10x10-pixel image is easier to work with, because it's big enough to click on. The difference in file size is insignificant.

Run Paint Shop Pro and create a new image. Make it 10 pixels high and 10 pixels wide and give it a transparent background

Export the image as a GIF. Select the 'Existing image or layer transparency' option

Set the number of colours to 2 and save the file

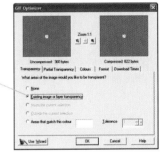

The advantage of using a spacer, rather than the Horizontal and Vertical spacing options (see page 59) is that you only add space where you want it, rather than on both sides of the image.

Switch to Namo WebEditor and use the spacer image to create blocks of empty space. If you want to separate two images, insert it between them. Stretch it to enlarge the gap

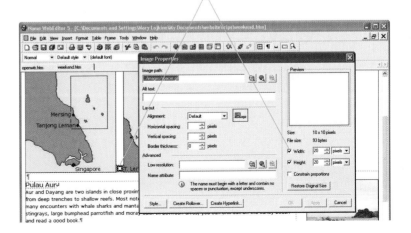

5   Spacer images are also useful for controlling the layout of tables. To separate a block of text from a column of pictures, insert an extra column, then use a spacer image to set the width

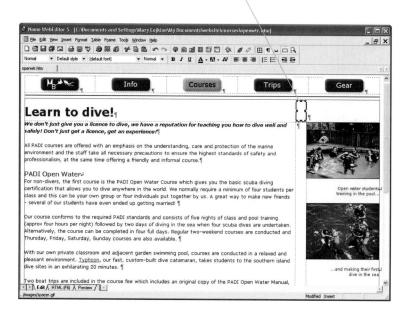

Using spacers produces more reliable results than setting the column widths and row heights in pixels.

A single spacer image can control both the width of a column and the height of a row. In the example shown, the spacer not only creates space between the pictures and the text, but also controls the height of the top row, creating extra space above the 'Learn to dive!' text (which has been aligned to the bottom of its cell).

Liquid tables

In the early days of the Web, text ran from one side of the browser window to the other. When the browser window got bigger, the lines got longer.

The table tags were added to HTML to make it easier for people to organise data into rows and columns. They were originally used to format price lists, schedules, financial reports and so on. However, people soon realised they could also be used to divide up the page and create magazine-style layouts, with multiple columns of text and separate areas for additional information and pictures. These days, most designers would crawl under their desks and weep if you told them to design an entire Web site without using tables.

Excessively complicated layouts place more demands on the viewer's Web browser and computer, so they take longer to appear. The pages are also difficult to edit.

The downside of tables is that they can give you too much control over the layout. If you aren't careful, you can lock down the structure so tightly that the page only looks right at the specific screen size it was designed for. When it's viewed on a smaller screen, the content spills over the edges, forcing your visitors to scroll left and right to read all the text. When it's viewed on a larger screen, there's lots of blank space.

800x600, looks great

640x480, too big

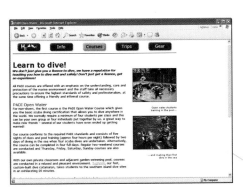

1,024x768, too small

Specifying table widths in pixels is okay for tables that are meant to be smaller than the smallest possible browser window – that is, up to 590 pixels wide.

Tables cause problems when you specify the width in pixels, rather than percentage terms, or lock down the entire structure using spacer images. The modern approach is to avoid these pitfalls and use 'liquid' tables that expand or contract as required.

There are two keys to creating liquid tables:

- Specify the width of the table as a percentage of the browser window. If it should fill the window, set the width to 100%

- Make sure that the width of at least one of the columns is unspecified. For example, the main section of the page shown below was laid out using a table with three columns. The width of the right-hand column is set by the photos; the width of the centre column is set using a spacer image. The left-hand column, containing the text, can expand or contract as required. The buttons also respace themselves

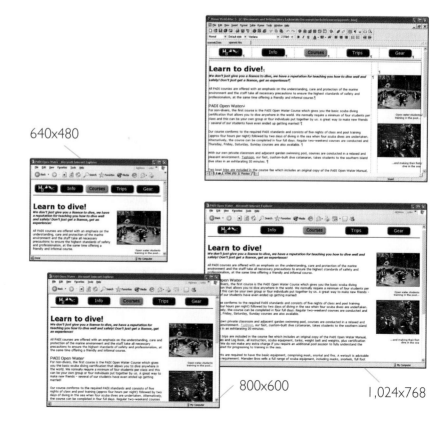

640x480

800x600

1,024x768

Image slicing

Slicing a graphic involves chopping it up into pieces and then reassembling the pieces in a table. There are three reasons for doing this:

- It enables you to put editable text into the blank areas around the edge of an irregularly shaped picture or logo. For example, this opening graphic is a single, large image. By slicing it into four pieces and discarding the top left one, it's possible to add text in an area that would usually be part of the image

Table cell containing text

NEWS FLASH:
Dive with sharks
at Rangiroa!

Table cells containing
pieces of the image

Marsden Bros
PADI Dive Centre

- It lets you use different degrees of compression on different areas of a large graphic. You can even use different formats

- It helps you create rollover effects efficiently. Instead of using two entire images, you can replace a small section of the first one

Creating slices

It's possible to slice a graphic manually, but you need to be very precise about the dimensions of each section. It's easier to use an image editor that has a built-in slicing function.

1 Run Paint Shop Pro and open the graphic you want to slice

2 Go to File>Export>Image Slicer

3 Select the Grid ⊞ tool and click on the preview image. Enter the number of rows and columns required

You can also use the Knife tool to subdivide individual slices.

4 Use the Arrow ⊠ tool to adjust the dividing lines

The slice that is currently selected is highlighted in green.

5 Select individual slices and link them to other Web pages (optional)

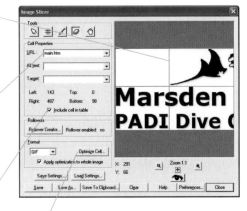

6 Exclude any slices that will be used for text

Select 'Apply optimization to whole image' to use the same settings for all the slices. Deselect this checkbox to optimise each slice separately.

7 Select the image format and click the Optimize Cell button to specify the settings

The image files for the slices end up in the same folder as the HTML document. If you want to move them, you'll need to edit the document to reflect their new locations.

8 Click the Save button to create a HTML document to hold the slices. Paint Shop Pro also creates an image file for each slice

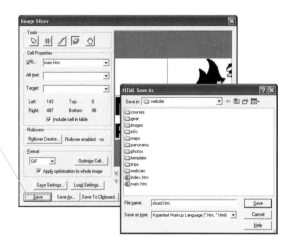

9 Open the HTML document in Namo WebEditor. You can either use it as the basis for a new Web page or select the entire table and copy it to an existing page

Tables that contain image slices should not be liquid (see page 147), they should be frozen solid. The width must be specified in pixels so the pieces are kept together, hard up against each other.

10 Add text to any cells that you've left empty for that purpose

Slicing and rollovers

Slicing enables you to create rollover effects more efficiently. It's useful when you have a large graphic and only want part of it to respond to the mouse.

Suppose you have an image of a fish, and you want it to flick its tail when the mouse passes over it. You could create two versions of the entire image:

However, the Web page will load more quickly if you slice the graphic and create a rollover that only replaces the tail section.

Open the first image in Paint Shop Pro and use the Slicer 🖉 tool to cut it into three pieces. Save it

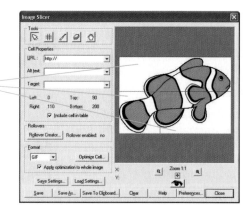

2 You need to cut out a piece of the second image that is the same size as the lower left slice. Open that slice in Paint Shop Pro and go to Image>Image Information to check its dimensions

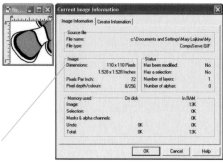

3 Open the second image and go to Image>Canvas Size. Enter the desired dimensions and make sure you are cropping pixels from the right areas – in this example, from the top and the right

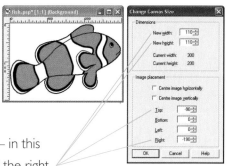

4 Export the cropped image as a GIF or JPEG

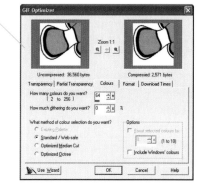

5 Switch to Namo WebEditor and open the HTML document containing the sliced image. Attach a hyperlink to each of the sections of the image, so you can add rollover effects

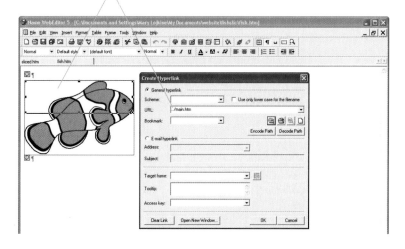

6 Right-click on the tail section and select Image Properties. Create a rollover effect using the image you prepared in Steps 3 and 4

You don't need to edit the code – you want to trigger the same effect each time, so you can use the same instructions.

7 Switch to HTML view and find the code for the rollover. Copy it into the `<a href>` tags for the other two sections of the image, so the rollover is triggered when the mouse touches any part of the image

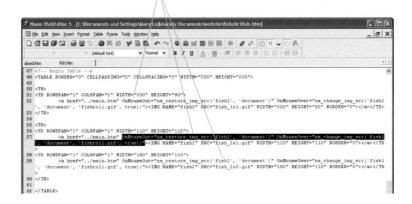

Slicing the image is worth the effort when you have a large file and you only want to change a small section of it. You can also trigger different effects from different sections of the graphic.

8 Test the page in your Web browser. The fish should flip its tail when the mouse passes over it

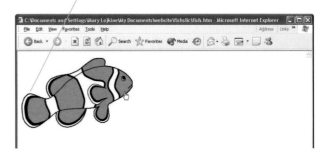

Animated GIFs

Animated GIFs are fun to make and a good way to grab people's attention. This chapter shows you how to animate text and simple illustrations. It also discusses the best ways to use animations without annoying your visitors.

Covers

Chapter Eight

Introduction

A GIF file can contain several different images that are displayed one after another, creating an animation.

Each frame adds to the size of the file, so it's best to keep the animation small and simple.

Movement draws the eye, so animations are a good way to attract people's attention. However, they can also be extremely irritating, so use them in moderation:

- Since the animation will be the most eye-catching item on the page, it should also be the most important item. It's okay to have an animated logo on the opening page of your Web site, but it's a mistake to include it on every page – it will distract people from your content. *Never* animate minor items of Web-page furniture such as bullets and rules

- Don't have more than one animation on a page. About the only exception to this is where you have two animations that are designed to work together. Don't have animations on every page, either – give people a rest

- Restrict the number of cycles. If you have other content on the same page as the animation, set it to loop a few times and then stop (see page 160). That way it attracts attention, then blends into the background once its job is done

- Since animations are saved in the GIF format, all the usual rules apply. If you reduce the pixel size of the frames, the number of colours and the amount of detail and shading, you'll get a smaller file that downloads more quickly

- Use your resources wisely. If you're just adding movement to your opening page, keep the animation small and simple. If you're creating a miniature movie that's original and entertaining, you can justify a larger file with more frames and more detail

Creating animations

Animated GIFs are normally created using specialist programs that give you control over features specific to animations, such as the delay between frames. Animation programs also make it easy to create transitions and special effects.

There are three options:

- A few image editors have built-in support for animations

- Some image editors come with companion programs that handle animations. For example, Jasc's Animation Shop is included with Paint Shop Pro

- Alternatively, you can get a standalone animation program

Most animation programs have basic painting and text tools that are adequate for creating simple animations. For more elaborate productions, you may want to create the frames in your image editor and then import them into the animation program.

When you start creating an animation, think about three things:

- **The size of the frames,** in pixels. Keep it small

- **The frame delay,** which is the time each frame is displayed for. It's usually measured in $1/100$ths of a second and a delay of $10/100$ths is a good starting point. That converts into 10 frames per second (fps), which gives you reasonably smooth movement (24fps gives you movie-quality animation, but your files will be correspondingly larger)

- **The overall plot.** What will happen in your animation? Which items will move, change colour, appear, disappear or interact? If you're making a complex animation, sketch out a storyboard showing the key scenes

Simple animations

One way to create an animation is to start with an existing graphic, then modify it using special effects.

1 Run Animation Shop and open one of your headings

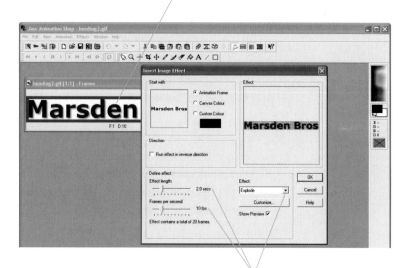

2 Go to Effects>Insert Image Effect. Select an effect from the drop-down list. Adjust the length and frame rate

3 Animation Shop adds frames to the animation. Use the scroll bar to flick through them

4 To preview the animation, go to View>Animation. Use the VCR-style controls to stop and start the animation

5 Go to Edit>Undo Insert Image Effect to remove the new frames and try something else

6 Go back to Paint Shop Pro and create a second image that's the same size as the first one. Copy it, then switch to Animation Shop. Go to Edit>Paste>After Current Frame to add it to the animation

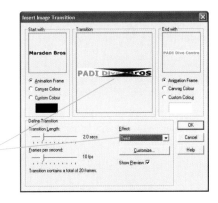

7 Scroll back to the first frame and click on it so it is selected. Go to Image> Insert Image Transition and select an effect. This time the effect converts the first frame into the second one

8 You might want to add another transition that turns the second image back into the first one. To do this, select the very first frame in the sequence and copy it. Select the last frame in the sequence, then go to Edit>Paste>After Current Frame. Select the second-to-last frame (the second image) and insert another transition

9 Preview the animation again

Animation controls

By default, all the frames are displayed for the same amount of time – typically $^{10}/_{100}$ ths of a second. Sometimes you'll want to increase the display time for some of the frames, so people can read your text or take in other details.

1 When you're applying special effects to text, you'll probably want the first and last frames to remain on the screen longer than the intermediate ones, so people have time to read your message. Select the first frame, then go to Animation>Frame Properties. Increase the display time. Do the same thing for the other key frames

2 To stop the animation after a fixed number of cycles, go to Animation> Animation Properties. Click the Looping tab and set the number of repeats

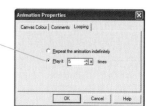

3 Depending on the circumstances, the browser may stop on either the first frame or the last frame, so it's a good idea to make them the same. Copy the first frame and paste it in at the end of the sequence, then adjust the display time accordingly

Saving animations

As with most other graphics, you should save the animation in a format that preserves as much information as possible, in case you want to edit it in the future. You can then save a second, compressed version for use on your Web site.

1 To save the animation, go to File>Save As. Select the Animation Shop Animation (.mng) format so you have a high-quality version of the file that you can come back to in the future

Creating a new animation gives you the option of checking the results and trying again if you aren't happy with the compressed file.

2 To create a version for your Web site, go to File> Optimization Wizard. Select the 'Animated GIF...' and 'Create a new animation...' options

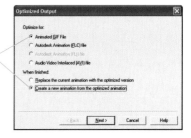

3 Adjust the slider according to your priorities

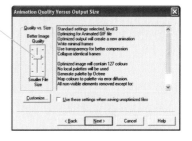

4 Check the size of the new animation, then click Finish and preview it

5 Go to File>Save As and save the animation in the GIF format

6 To add the animation to your Web page, insert it as if it were a regular image (see page 79)

Animating movement

Animating movement requires more patience. Create the basic images in your image editor, then string them together with your animation program, adjusting their position from frame to frame.

1 Run Paint Shop Pro and open the image you want to animate

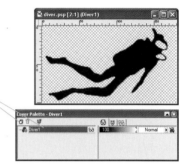

2 Drag the existing layer on to the Create Layer button to duplicate it

3 Edit the new layer to create a second version of the image. Here the legs are being rotated to make the diver kick. Reduce the opacity of either the top or the bottom layer so you can compare the two images

4 Continue until you have several versions of the basic image

5 Run Animation Shop and go to File> New. If your subject is going to move around the frame, make the animation bigger than your basic image

6 Switch to Paint Shop Pro and copy the first image, then switch to Animation Shop. Go to Edit>Paste>Into Selected Frame (or press Ctrl+E) to paste and position the first image

7 Go to Animation>Insert Frames> Empty to add some more frames

'Onionskin' is a term borrowed from traditional animation. The Onionskin option simulates the effect of drawing a frame on translucent paper, with the previous frame underneath for reference.

8 Go to View>Onionskin>Settings. Enable the Onionskin Preview and set the number of Overlays to 2

9 Scroll along to the second frame and click on it so it is selected. Copy and paste the second image. Use the faint image of the first frame to judge the correct position

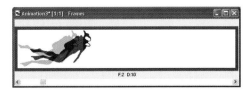

10 Continue pasting in images until the animation is complete

11 Preview, optimise and save the animation (see page 161)

Other types of animation

Animated GIFs are popular because they are easy to create and can be viewed in most Web browsers without any additional software. However, the files can get quite large.

The other common format for animations is Macromedia's Flash format. Flash animations are created using vector images (see page 21), which are stored very efficiently using mathematical equations. Flash animations can also be interactive – they can be triggered by the viewer's mouse movements or other actions.

One disadvantage of the Flash format is that people need to install additional (free) software to see your animations. Although many Internet users have the Flash plug-in, some people are reluctant to install extra software. People in corporate environments may not be allowed to. Another disadvantage is that the software required to create Flash animations is more expensive than most GIF animation programs.

For more information about the Flash format, visit Macromedia's Web site at `http://www.macromedia.com/`

Panoramas

A 360-panorama is a wrap-around image that makes you feel as if you're standing in the middle of a scene. You can look left and right and zoom in or out, exploring the location at your leisure. This chapter explains how to create these sophisticated and interesting images.

Covers

Chapter Nine

Introduction

A 360-degree panorama is a long, thin photograph that has been wrapped around on itself so the ends join up. When you view it, you feel as if you're standing in the middle of the scene. You can turn to your left or your right, just as you would in real life, until you've seen everything there is to see.

A panorama is an excellent way to record an area of outstanding natural beauty. Rather than sharing individual, isolated views, you can capture the entire scene and enable people to immerse themselves in it. However, you don't have to restrict yourself to the great outdoors. Some of the best panoramas depict the interiors of churches, historic houses and concert halls. If you're running a restaurant or hotel, you can create panoramic images of your facilities, so people know exactly what to expect.

To create a panoramic image, you take a series of overlapping photographs, then stitch them together. Usually the final image is cylindrical, but it's also possible to create spherical panoramas that provide a 360-degree field of view in every direction, enabling people to look up and down as well as right and left.

The two most common formats for panoramas are IPIX and QuickTime Virtual Reality (also called QuickTime VR or QTVR).

- **The IPIX format** was developed by Internet Pictures (`http://www.ipix.com/`). IPIX panoramas are spherical, so people can look in every direction. You need a camera with a special fish-eye lens to capture the photos and you have to use Internet Picture's own software to stitch them together. You're also charged per image

- **QuickTime VR** was developed by Apple (`http://www.apple.com/quicktime/qtvr/`). It doesn't offer the same field of view as IPIX, but you can use an ordinary camera with a regular lens. Also, there are several third-party programs that can save images in this format, so you aren't restricted to Apple's (Mac only) QuickTime VR Authoring Studio

Special software is required to view IPIX and QuickTime VR images, so people may have to install a browser plug-in the first time they visit your Web site. In both cases the plug-in is free.

Equipment and software

The rest of this chapter explains how to create QuickTime VR panoramas. The software is inexpensive and you don't need any special equipment, so they're the best choice for beginners.

You need four things to create a QuickTime VR panorama:

- **A camera.** A digital camera is ideal, because you'll need to take about a dozen photographs. Capturing them digitally cuts down on the expense. However, you can achieve the same results using a conventional camera and a scanner. Either way, the wider the lens, the fewer photographs you need and the better the results

- **A tripod.** You don't absolutely have to have one, but it's much easier to join your photographs if they're all taken from exactly the same spot. Ideally you want a tripod with a pan-and-tilt head, so you can rotate the camera without tipping it up or down

- **A spirit level,** so you can check that the tripod is level. If your camera has a hot shoe for an external flash, you can get a little spirit level that sits in the shoe

For detailed reviews of image-stitching programs, visit the Panoguide Web site at http://www.panoguide.com/

- **A stitching program** that can find the points where your photographs overlap and blend them together, creating a single image with no visible seams. Some image editors are able to stitch photographs and save them in the QuickTime VR format. If yours isn't, you'll need a specialist stitching program such as ImageAssembler from PanaVue (http://www.panavue.com/)

Taking the pictures

When you take a single photograph, you can adjust the framing to leave out lampposts and rubbish bins. With a panorama, you don't have the same flexibility. However, it isn't the small details that make or break your image, it's the overall view.

To create a good panorama, you need a location that provides all-around interest. There aren't many places that have arresting views in all directions, but you should be able to find a spot that has something worth seeing at several points around the circle. Try to get out into the open – if you're backed up against a wall, you'll only have 180 degrees of view.

When you take the photographs, the camera must be absolutely level. If you tilt it up or down, you won't be able to stitch the images into a cylinder. Make sure the photographs overlap by between 20 and 50 per cent, so the software can find areas that match and line up the images. Avoid moving objects such as people and vehicles, or keep them in the centre of the frame so they only appear once. Finally, try to take your pictures while the sun is high in the sky or obscured by cloud, so the scene is evenly lit.

You'll end up with a series of overlapping photographs:

Checking the lens

Even if you know the focal length of your lens, you'll usually get better results by letting the program estimate it.

Most stitching programs need to know the focal length of your lens. Often they can estimate it for you after examining a couple of photographs from your series.

1 Run ImageAssembler and go to File > New Project. Select the Lens Wizard option

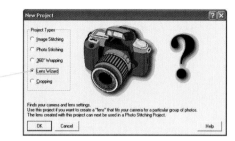

2 Specify the number of photos – three, ideally – and tell the program how they are arranged

3 Click the Images tab, then click the Add button and select three of the images from your series

...cont'd

The Flag Assistant helps you place the flags accurately. It compares the areas around the two flags and moves the second one to a matching position.

4 Activate the Flag Assistant 🏴 by clicking its button, then place the flags at distinctive, matching points along the overlaps

5 Click the Full Run 🏃 button to stitch the images and measure the focal length of the lens

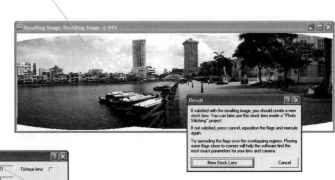

6 If you're happy with the stitched image, save the lens details for use in your stitching project

Stitching the images

Before you stitch your photographs, perform any basic editing that is required (see page 102). Make sure all the images have the same dimensions. If you are using photographs from a digital camera, you may need to resize them so the final image isn't unworkably large. Try reducing them to 800x600 pixels.

1 Run ImageAssembler and go to File>New Project. Select Photo Stitching and tell it how the photographs are arranged

Adding the first image twice makes it easier to stitch the ends – see page 173.

2 Click the Images tab, then click the Add button and select your photos. Add the first one twice, once at the start and once at the end

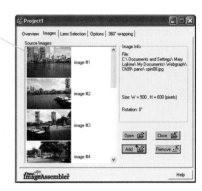

3 Click the Lens Selection tab and select the lens you created earlier (see page 169)

4 Click the Options tab. Select 'Automatic stitch…' and Spherical projection

5 Click the Preview Run 👁 button and conduct a test stitch. If the result is satisfactory, skip ahead to Step 9

6   If some of the joins aren't quite right, go back to the Options page and select 'Manual stitch with 1 flag'

7   Find the first two photos. Turn on the Flag Assistant and line up the flags on matching points

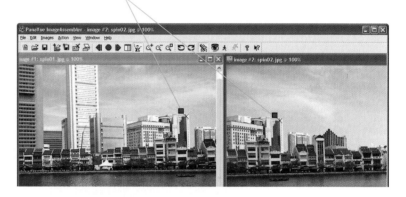

8   Repeat for the second and third images, and so on, until you've placed flags along all the joins. Try another preview run

If there are minor imperfections in the final image, go to File>Save Image As and save it in a format your image editor supports. Edit the image, then go back to ImageAssembler to stitch the ends together.

9   Once you're happy with the preview image, click the Full Run button to produce a high-resolution image

Joining the ends

To turn the 'flat' panorama into a 360-degree image, you need to trim the edges and join the ends.

1   If you've just stitched the image, go back to the Project Window. Click the 360° Wrapping tab, then click the 'Bring the resulting image…' button

2   To stitch a saved image from a previous session, start a new project. Select 360° Wrapping, then open the image

Try to put the join in the middle of the first photo (the one you added at both ends).

3   Zoom in and position the flags at the ends of the image on matching points

4   Zoom out and use the mouse to adjust the top and bottom of the cropping box

Keeping a copy of the panorama in a flat format makes things easier if you need to edit it. If the final version is too large (in file-size terms) to use on-line, you can resize the flat image, then save it in QTVR format again.

5   Click the Full Run button to crop the image

6   Go to File>Save Image As and save the image in a 'flat' format that is supported by your image editor, such as TIFF or PNG

7 Save the image
again, this time
in QuickTime VR
format (with a
.mov extension)

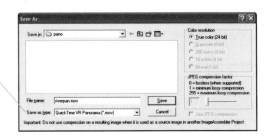

8 Set the image quality (which
determines the compression level)
and the size of the viewing window.
Click OK to save the file

You'll need
QuickTime
installed to
view your
panorama.
Get it from `http://www.`
`apple.com/quicktime/`
`download/`

9 To view your panorama, use
Windows Explorer to locate the
file, then double-click on it

10 Hold down the mouse button
and drag the mouse left and right
to move around. Press Shift to zoom in and Ctrl to zoom out

Inserting panoramas

Panoramas are inevitably large files. It's best to add them to your pages as linked files and warn people about their size.

Linking to the panorama is just like linking directly to a GIF or JPEG image – see page 112.

1 Create a Web page with some text describing the image

2 Link the text directly to the file containing the panorama

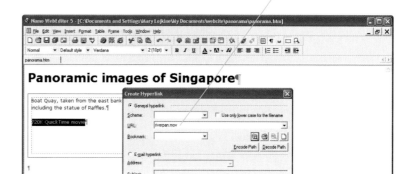

3 Tell people they'll need QuickTime to view the file(s) and add a link to Apple's Web site (see the Don't Forget, opposite). You might also want to tell them how to move around the panorama

4 When someone clicks the link to the panorama, it'll be downloaded and displayed in the centre of their browser window

Smaller panoramas

You can also create panoramas from just two or three images. This trick is useful when you're trying to photograph something that's simply too wide (or too tall) for a single shot. Take your photos, stitch them and save the final image as a JPEG.

The photo is only scaled if it is displayed on its own, rather than as part of a Web page.

If your final image is too wide or too tall for the browser window, Internet Explorer 6 scales it to fit (other browsers display scroll bars). To see the full-size image, visitors have to hover the mouse over the image, then click the Expand to Regular Size button that appears in the lower right corner.

Automatic Image Resizing was a new feature in Internet Explorer 6 and many people don't know that their browser is shrinking some images. If you want to display wide or tall images, it's a good idea to tell IE6 users how to expand them.

Images for e-mail

The graphics you've created for your Web site can also be used to brighten up your e-mails. Whether you're communicating with people via your site or by e-mail, you can present your information in a consistent, easily recognisable style.

Covers

Chapter Ten

Introduction

E-mail used to be a text-only application. Whatever your message, you had to convey it using plain, unformatted text. If you were absolutely desperate to include a picture, you had to create it using letters, numbers and punctuation:

```
:-)                    Person smiling (turn the book clockwise)

    ///
<°)))))<      Fish
    \\
```

Over the last few years e-mail programs and Web browsers have become more closely integrated and now it's possible to use HTML in your messages. You can format your text, making it bold, italic or coloured, and you can include graphics. Your e-mail messages can look just as good as your Web pages.

HTML formatting is useful for newsletters and promotional messages. More attractive messages are more likely to be read and pictures make it easier to tell a story or highlight a product. However, formatted messages also have their drawbacks:

- Older mail programs can't interpret the formatting and may display a baffling mess of HTML tags

- Pictures make your message larger, so it takes longer to download. Since speed is one of the best features of e-mail, many people find this annoying

- HTML mail can be associated with security problems such as viruses and worms, so some people are suspicious of it

Because of these problems, you should only send formatted mail to people who have indicated that they're willing to accept it. If you're sending out a regular newsletter, it's a good idea to create two versions, one plain and one formatted, and let people sign up for the version they prefer.

Formatting messages also takes time. Given the potential problems, you need to decide whether it's worth the effort. Sometimes it is, but sometimes plain text is just as effective.

Backgrounds

The easiest way to jazz up your messages is by adding background images. It's the Internet equivalent of using coloured writing paper.

1 Follow the instructions on page 95 to create a background image in the GIF or JPG format

In Netscape Messenger, click the Options button to access the Format settings. To add a background image, go to Format>Page Colors and Properties.

2 Create a new mail message. Make sure you are in HTML mode – in Outlook Express, go to Format and check that Rich Text (HTML) is selected

3 Go to Format>Background> Picture. Click the Browse button and locate your background image. It is added to your message

4 Before you send the message, go to the Format menu and check that Send Pictures With Message is selected

Headings and logos

Adding a heading or logo at the top of your messages creates a virtual letterhead.

1 Follow the instructions on pages 69 to 77 to create a heading or logo. Don't make it too wide, because many people view e-mail messages in relatively small windows

2 Create a new mail message. Make sure you're in HTML mode

When you add a picture to an e-mail message, you have many of the same options that you have when you add it to a Web page. You can add Alt text (see page 56) and/or a border (page 58) and adjust the alignment (page 57) and spacing (page 59).

3 Go to Insert> Picture or click the Insert Picture  button. Click the Browse button and find your image

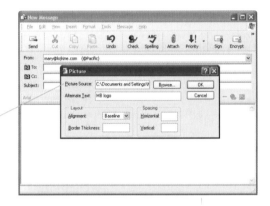

In Netscape Messenger, go to Insert> Image to add an image. You can also click the Insert Object button and select Insert Image.

4 The image is inserted. Add your text to complete the message

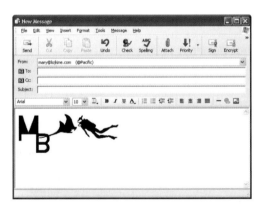

5 Check that Format>Send Pictures with Message is selected before you click the Send button

Stationery

Inserting background images and logos into every message soon becomes tedious. Outlook Express offers a better alternative: you can save all your images and settings as part of a 'stationery' file. You can then select an appropriate 'piece' of stationery each time you compose a message.

The easiest way to create stationery is with the Stationery Wizard.

1 Create your images, then copy the files into the C:\Program Files\Common Files\Microsoft Shared\Stationery folder

2 Run Outlook Express and go to Tools>Options. Click on the Compose tab. In the Stationery subsection, click the Create New button

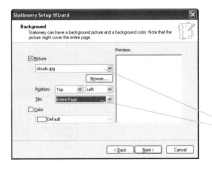

3 The Wizard prompts you for a background picture or colour. If you want the image to repeat, set Tile to Entire Page

The Wizard only lets you insert one image. If you want to have a background and a heading, you have to edit the file later on – see page 183.

4 A heading or logo shouldn't be tiled, because you only want it to appear once. You still insert it as a background image, but you'll need to set Tile to Do Not Tile

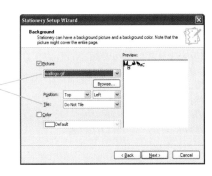

Pick a font most people will have – see page 69.

5 Choose a standard font for this stationery and specify its size and colour

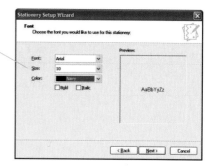

6 Adjust the margins so the text misses your heading

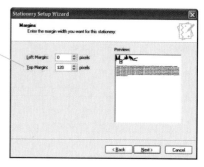

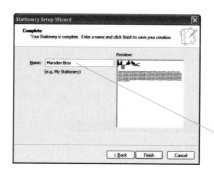

7 Give your design a name and click Finish to save it

Netscape Messenger uses templates instead of stationery.
To create one, create a new message. Insert your images, plus any text that should appear in every message, then go to File>Save As>Template.
*   To use the template, go back to the main Messenger window. Select the Templates folder, then double-click on the template.*

8 To create a message using your stationery, click the arrow next to the Create Mail button. If your design appears in the drop-down list, select it. If it doesn't, choose the Select Stationery option for a complete list of designs

Editing stationery

Netscape Messenger's templates aren't stored as HTML files, so you have to edit them within Messenger.

There's nothing special about a stationery file. It's just a HTML document, like a regular Web page, so you use your HTML editor to make changes.

Run Namo WebEditor and open your stationery file

2 The logo is inserted as a background image. If you want to add a background texture or pattern, you need to change things around. Switch to HTML mode and look at the code at the top of the page

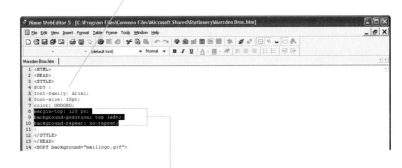

3 Delete the special codes that control the margins and the background repeat

4 Switch back to Edit mode and go to File>Document Properties. Select your background image

5 Reinsert the logo as a regular image

6 If you have text that you want to include in every message, you can add that to your stationery as well

7 Save the file, then switch to Outlook Express and create a test message to check that everything is in the right place:

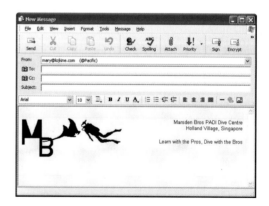

Mailouts and newsletters

If you want to use HTML formatting in a mailout or newsletter, the simplest option is to create a Web page in your HTML editor, then e-mail it. You may be able to dispatch it directly from your HTML editor. If not, you can copy everything to a mail message.

There are a few things to be aware of when you're designing documents for transmission by e-mail:

- **Minimise the image load.** If people think your Web pages are taking too long to download, they can click the Stop button and abort the transfer. If you send them a very large e-mail message, there's little they can do except grind their teeth and wait for it to arrive. Use as few images as possible and compress them aggressively

- **Send the images with the message.** It's possible to create messages that simply include references to images on your Web site. When the message is opened, the e-mail program finds and downloads the images and adds them to the message. The problem with this approach is that many people log on to the Internet to collect their mail, then disconnect and read their messages. When they open a message that includes references to on-line images, their e-mail program prompts them to reconnect. If they don't, they won't see the pictures. Either option is annoying: messages with missing graphics are unappealing, but no-one wants to open a new connection just for a couple of images

Test your mailout in as many different mail programs as you can.
It's also a good idea to ask your readers for feedback, because you can never be sure what will annoy people.

- **Be careful with tables.** Mail messages that are too wide for their allotted window are even more irritating than Web pages that are too wide for the viewer's screen. Specify the widths of your tables in percentage terms, rather than pixels, so they can adjust themselves to fill the available space

- **Don't be too clever.** Mailouts shouldn't contain scripts or animations, or have elaborate layouts. People value the ease and speed of e-mail, so don't make it difficult and slow

In short, keep it small and keep it simple.

Designing a mailout

It's best to design your mailouts from scratch. That way you're forced to consider the relevance and size of each image. If nothing else, sheer laziness should encourage you to keep things simple!

1 Run your HTML editor and design your mailout

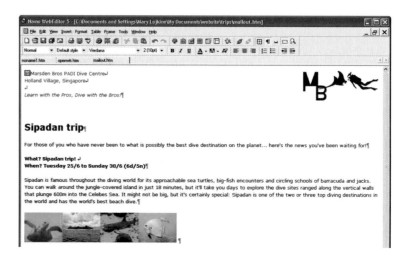

If your HTML editor doesn't have this option, try selecting everything on the page and copying it. Switch to your e-mail program and paste the information into a new message. If that doesn't work, you may have to use your mail program to create the mailout, rather than your HTML editor.

It's a good idea to send a test version to yourself, just to be sure that everything is correct

2 Go to File>Send E-mail. The page is transferred to a new message. Check the layout and tweak it if necessary. Fill in the subject and address(es) and double-check that the pictures will be included

Index

24-bit colour   24, 35, 41, 70
360-degree panoramas. *See* Panoramas
3D effects. *See* Cutout effect; Drop shadows

<a href> tag   60
Add Noise effect   96
Alignment
   In table cells   64, 108, 146
   Of graphics   53, 57, 107
   Of headings   80
   Of horizontal rules   90
Alpha channels   71–72
Alt text   13, 56, 61, 79, 124
Animation programs   16, 157
Animation Shop   157
Animations
   Creating   158, 162
   Frame delay   157, 160
   Inserting   161
   Introduction   156
   Looping   160
   Saving   161
Anti-aliasing   34, 42, 70, 77, 141
Apple (Web site)   166
Artifacts   38
Automatic image resizing   176

Backgrounds
   Coloured   92, 141
   For e-mail   179, 181, 183
   Photographic   115

Repeating graphics   93
Seamless textures and patterns   95, 141
Sidebars   94
Beckham, Victoria (Web site)   12
Bitmap graphics   21
Bits   24
Borders
   For images   58, 61, 106
   For tables   63–64
   For thumbnails   110
Browser-safe palette   28, 30, 32, 35, 67, 76
Bullets   23, 91
Buttons
   Adding text   85
   Caching   23
   Creating   83
   Inserting   87
   Introduction   82
   Linking from   87
   Rollovers   129
Bytes   24

Cache   23
Canvas size   111, 153
Captions   56, 64, 108
Cell padding   63, 108
Cell spacing   63, 108, 111
Centring
   Buttons   88
   Graphics   57
   Headings   80
   Tables   87
Clip-art   11, 66
Colour balance   103
Colours   24, 28, 30, 32, 42, 67, 71
Compression   41
   JPEG   38, 41–42, 105
   Lossless   36

D

E

F

G